Ditch the Doubt

The Modern Witch Way to create clarity and feel great about your decisions… every time

Rebecca-Anuwen

Design by GW Illustration
www.GrantWickham.co.uk

 RebeccaAnuwen.com

 facebook.com/YourSherosJourney

 instagram.com/YourSherosJourney

Dedication

This book is dedicated to anyone who has ever doubted themselves when they've wanted or needed to make a decision.

Testimonials

It's so much easier to let things go

"I hadn't realised what a difference developing a relationship with my energy would make.

I understand now how much I absorb other people's energy, and Rebecca's daily practices have given me the tools to quickly and easily clear away what isn't mine and keep my boundaries firm. So much gratitude for that.

I'm finding it so much easier to let things go as well, and that's very empowering.

I've stopped worrying so much about what other people think – and about time too!

It's crazy what we absorb and carry with us for years and years and years... I love starting my day this way."

~ Shirley

It just makes sense

"I'm generally a very peaceful person, and I'm often described as cool, calm and collected. However, I have an unfortunate habit of allowing those around me to affect my energy.

Rebecca's SACRED practices have been a godsend.

Working with the practices has given me tips, tricks and a morning ritual that I can tailor to give me exactly what I need. It grounds my energy, solidifies my boundaries and protects what is most precious to me: my inner peace.

This has helped me in my relationships with not only friends and family, but also with myself.

Rebecca is incredibly gifted with the ability to explain things in a way that clicks. It just makes sense. Her spirit is also fabulously warm and giving. You will not be disappointed."

~ Audrey Eckler

Life-changing for me

"Rebecca's SACRED practices have been really life-changing for me.

I know how important it is to keep up with energy hygiene, but knowing isn't doing!

Doing this work with Rebecca has completely changed how I feel about taking care of my energy.

For the first time in my life, I feel consistently grounded. I know what my baseline energy should feel like when it's clear, so now I also know when I need to clear it.

I've always been an energetic sponge, taking on other people's energy without even being aware of it. I've now mostly stopped doing this accidentally, yet I can still easily share energy for my work with others if I decide to.

Rebecca has such a fun teaching style, and has shared so many different tips and techniques. I now feel confident that I can clear my energy quickly, no matter where I am or what (if any) tools I have with me."

~ Tasha B

Proactively and consciously choose

"I don't think I realised the benefits of Rebecca's energy health work until I stopped the daily practices while travelling!

The impact far outweighs the short time it takes me to ground my energy every day.

More than anything, it's empowering. It's a way to proactively and consciously choose what I bring into my day.

It sets an intention. It provides focus. And it stops the reactivity to everything around me."

~ Janice Radomsky

I feel a deeper peace than I ever have before

"The SACRED practices feel like the missing pieces of a puzzle.

I've journaled, exercised and eaten well; but sometimes, no matter how 'well' I do, I can't seem to let go of those old nagging feelings.

After doing the practices over the last 45 days, I feel a deeper peace than I ever have before. I know what's mine and what's not. I've established my boundaries, and it has become so much easier to simply let things go.

This has truly been an invaluable and life-changing experience! Thank you, Rebecca!"

~ Mackenzie Ledford

Table of Contents

Introduction

Do you struggle with decision-making?

So many of the clients I work with find it hard to make clear, confident decisions and then stand behind them.

Some of them struggle to decide on anything in the first place.

What if they get it wrong? What if they forget to consider something important? What if, regardless of what they decide, they end up hurting or upsetting someone they care about?

So they sit on the fence and end up making the decision not to decide.

Others make a choice and feel good about it in the moment.

But as the day goes on, they begin to doubt themselves. Was that really what they wanted? Was it honestly realistic? Perhaps they should have chosen a better option?

That's when they start asking themselves:

- Is this really the right choice for me?
- What will XYZ think of that choice?
- Can I really do that?
- Isn't that a bit out of reach for me?

- Am I qualified enough / intelligent enough / rich enough / old enough / young enough / thin enough / funny enough / serious enough?
- When I tried that in the past, it didn't work. Am I stupid for thinking it will work this time?
- Am I just setting myself up to fail?
- Should I ask a few people and see what they think?

Or perhaps they're confident in their decision *until* they speak to a friend or family member who immediately makes them wonder what on earth they were thinking.

So if decision-making isn't your strong suit, you're not alone.

Good decisions require good information

People have written a *lot* about how to make confident decisions. The problem is that much of what's been written focusses on rational, logical ways to choose between different options.

There's nothing wrong with listening to what your logical mind has to say. It's okay to consider its 'voice of reason' as ONE source of information.

But if you make that part of your mind your only source of guidance, you're missing out on a wealth of valuable information.

To get the full story, you need to listen to your intuition as well. You need to value everything it says – its small, quiet whispers and occasional clear messages that something's wrong – just as highly as the voice of your intellect (if not more so).

Unfortunately, our culture teaches us to ignore and second-guess our intuitions.

And even if we don't actively distrust the idea of intuitive messages, many of us are so busy and overwhelmed that the clutter of our lives simply drowns them out.

Unless we create some space in our lives, we can't hear the valuable guidance our intuitions provide.

The Modern Witch way to create space in your life

In this book, I've collected three of the most powerful practices I know of to help create the space you need to hear the voice of your intuition.

- **The SACRED practice** is one I like to use in the morning to start my day fresh, grounded and energetically aligned. It helps me to distinguish all the voices, messages, ideas and energies that are mine from those that aren't... Then it helps me to release anything that isn't mine, so I can make clear, conscious choices for the day ahead.

- **The GRACE practice** is one I like to use in the evening or at the end of the week to create closure. It helps me to let go of everything I've accumulated that isn't mine. It also allows me a moment to recognise and reflect on all that I've done and achieved (or chosen not to do). That means I can start the new day or week with an energetic reset – feeling refreshed, calm and clear.

- **The Sacred Pause practice** is a quick, simple, in-the-moment practice that I can use anywhere at any time to create space in my life when I need it.

We'll talk more about the individual steps that make up the SACRED and GRACE practices (and why I've called them that) in the chapters for each practice.

For the meantime, know that these practices may look a little complicated when you first read about them. Once you start doing them regularly though, you'll find that the first two only take 5-10 minutes each, and the Sacred Pause practice can take as little as a few moments.

And once you've made these practices a regular part of your life, you can expect to:

- make decisions with clarity and ease (and stick with them)
- believe in and trust yourself and your choices more
- feel more aligned with who you truly are as you cut out the noise of other people's judgements and expectations
- confidently understand and interpret the intuitive messages, insights and feelings you receive
- feel lighter and more joyful
- tap into a greater sense of flow in your life

How to use this book

To get the most out of this book, I recommend reading right through it once from start to finish. This will give you a general feel for each practice and how you might adapt it to suit your needs and lifestyle.

Then, decide on the practice you want to try first and re-read that practice before you go ahead and try it. Simply knowing what to do isn't enough – you've got to actually *do* it.

They're called 'practices' because they're designed to be practised!

It's a bit like deciding to go to the gym because you want to get stronger or move more comfortably. You can read all the books you like on good workout form, and learn which moves help which muscles and which stretches free up which joints. But until you actually rock up to the gym, stow your gear in a locker and get out onto the floor, you're not going to see any progress.

And, much like with a gym membership, it's not enough to go once (or even once a month) and then expect to see dramatic benefits. To get stronger or more flexible, you need to train regularly – at least two or three times a week, if not more.

It's exactly the same with these practices. Plus, much like with gym training, the more often you practise them, the more quickly they begin to feel natural and easy. They stop feeling like a big, dramatic hassle that demands a lot of preparation and figuring out. Instead, they just become a natural part of your day that you slide into.

However, if you're short on time right now, decide what's most important to you by asking yourself:

- Do you feel confused, overwhelmed and unable to make a clear choice that you'll stick to?

- Do you feel weighed down by expectations and judgements, and want to clear the heaviness to feel lighter and freer?

- Do you need just a moment to pause, rest and really understand how you're feeling?

If you're feeling confused about a choice you need to make, jump straight into the first chapter in the SACRED Practice section. This practice will leave you feeling aligned, clear and on purpose, allowing you to make confident, conscious choices.

If you're feeling overwhelmed or simply bleucch, head to the GRACE practice. There, you'll learn how to reset your energy and come back to your own centre, leaving you feeling fresher, clearer and ready for whatever you need to do next.

Or, if you find you can't 'catch your breath', head to the Sacred Pause practice. That will offer you a moment to come back to your centre, and give you some space to breathe and feel again.

Finally, after you've read through the relevant information, head to the videos at www.RebeccaAnuwen.com/DecisionBonuses. In them, I'll walk you through each of the practices step-by-step for even greater clarity.

Don't let the simplicity fool you

As a culture, we tend to value highly complex things... but complex doesn't always mean better.

In reality, I've found that the simple things are often the most effective. Maybe that's because when things are easy, we're more likely to do them.

I've also found that the more rigidly structured and one-size-fits-all something is, the less helpful I'm likely to find it.

So I deliberately created these practices to be as simple – and flexible – as possible. They're not strict process diagrams that you need to follow to the letter. Instead, they're flexible support structures that you can build on and work with to create something unique that's perfect for you.

Before we talk about the practices themselves, though, let's quickly go over some background concepts.

Background Concepts

Magical Decision-Making

It might seem strange to talk about magic and decision-making in the same breath.

After all – magic, by definition, seems like something mystical. It belongs to the hidden realms. It's something that can't be explained by science or logic. Meanwhile, decision-making is about weighing up facts and choosing the most rational option... or so we're told.

But the reality is that magic is about creating change – usually because you either want more of something in your life, or want to be free of something. For example, you might want to be more confident, or to rid yourself of unwanted attention.

The thing is that change only happens when you align your thoughts, feelings and desires (in other words, intentionally direct your energy) towards it. And another word for aligning and directing thoughts and energy – sometimes using tools like candles, crystals and herbs – is 'magic'.

Regardless of whether or not you use tools, though, you still have to align your actions with your intentions to create real change.

The same is true when you need to decide between various options. If you want to feel confident that you've made 'the right' choice, you need to identify the option that best honours every aspect of you. Then you need to align your thoughts, feelings and desires with that option.

Only when you've done this will your actions align with your choice. Only then will you do whatever you need to do to see the decision through.

In other words, both magic and clear decision-making require you to identify and then align with what's truly important to you. If you don't know what you want, or you're not willing to take action once you know it, you'll never get the outcome you desire.

And that's true, whether you call what you're doing 'magic' or not.

Let's talk about what magic really is

There's often fear or uncertainty around magic, and misunderstandings about what it is. For example, people think that they need to be born into magic, have a magical lineage or have special skills.

But magic is just the ability to tap into the rhythms that flow around and within you.

After that, it's just using those rhythms to create change or influence the world around you.

Both the quality of your energy and your connection to your own inner power will influence the quality of the magic you bring to and express in the world. And, not coincidentally, they'll also affect the quality of the decisions you make.

A 'so-so' connection with, and belief and trust in, your own magic will inevitably create 'so-so' results. A clear, confident connection with your own magic will create clear, confident results.

Of course, some people can access their magic with greater ease than others, just like some people naturally connect to their intuition more easily. But both magic and intuition are available to everyone.

And both play an important role in making clear, confident decisions.

Sacred tools aren't magical

Before we talk about using magic to help you make good decisions, let's take a moment to discuss sacred magical tools.

There's nothing inherently wrong with magical tools. I absolutely love them.

I have a *particular* love of cauldrons – to the point that I won't even admit how many I have. I've also made several wands, incense fans and brooms.

My favourites, though, are divination tools. I have scores of oracle and Tarot decks, not to mention runes, Ogham staves and charms for Charm Casting. On top of all those, I have crystals and herbs and oils.

And I love to use ALL of these tools in my spell work and magic.

But... I don't really need any of them.

Neither do you.

All these tools are great to have. They're fun to work with, and they can help you to connect with and direct your energy.

But you're the one who actually brings the magic to any working you do. Your magic is always there inside of you – and you bring it to every tool you use.

You bring the magic, because you ARE the magic.

Ritual and magic

For the longest time, people have found comfort in ritual, and have used it – knowingly or not – as a vehicle for magic.

After all, ritual allows us to focus and direct our energy and intention. And, as we discussed at the beginning of this chapter, that's all that magic really is.

Ritual can also guide us into a deeper relationship with ourselves and the world around us.

So it's not surprising that ritual can help you to both make decisions you feel clear and confident about, and then take action based on those decisions.

I invite you to use the sacred practices in this book as magical rituals in whatever way works best for you. Use them to pause and really hear what your soul and intuition are whispering to you. Then use them to direct your energy in ways that align with those messages to bring you peace and certainty.

Of course, before you can listen for the voice of your intuition, it helps to have a clear sense of what intuition is and how it works...

Intuition: It's Not What You Think (Probably)

What is intuition?

I define intuition as 'your immediate, often unexplained, understanding of something'.

You might call it 'trusting your gut', 'tuning into your sixth sense' or 'listening to your feelings'.

It's that quiet voice whose message you just *know* to be true when it speaks to you. Maybe it's a whisper, or a feeling pulling you forward. Or perhaps it's the quiet voice that encourages you to make the changes you desire or that tells you to try again.

Your intuition usually comes as a moment of clarity or a deep, immediate knowing about something that you can't logically explain.

Maybe you walked into a room and just knew that something wasn't right. No-one said anything wrong, and nothing looked obviously out of place... but you just knew. Or perhaps you felt a strong internal 'call' to follow a certain desire, and instantly *knew* that it was what you needed to do next in your life.

A few years ago, I interviewed Becky Walsh, who said that we have two types of intuition: heart intuition and gut intuition.

Heart intuition is what pulls us forward. It shows us whether actions are or aren't aligned for us. Perhaps you feel this kind of intuition as a deep knowing that it's time to change jobs, start a new career or leave a relationship.

Meanwhile, gut intuition moves us 'back' away from danger. You might experience this kind of intuition when you meet someone who just feels 'off' or get a sense that you shouldn't walk down a certain road. That's your gut intuition keeping you safe.

Regardless of the form it takes, intuition is a type of inner wisdom and guidance that complements your intellectual, logical reasoning.

And it's almost impossible to make good decisions without factoring its guidance into your choice.

Not every internal voice is your intuition

Of course, sometimes the messages from the 'voices in your head' aren't helpful ones.

Maybe your inner voice insists that you've done something wrong (again), that you're (still) not good enough or that you don't deserve what you desire (and never will).

Or perhaps it insists that something you feel a soul calling to do is far too dangerous and would never work out – even though you know intellectually that it's safe.

The examples in the previous section were your intuition communicating with you. The voices above in this section are – respectively – your inner critic and your trauma-based fear speaking.

How can you tell which is which?

You tell by paying attention to the quality of the messages you receive.

Intuition is subtle and nuanced. Its messages are generally quiet, and either emotionally neutral or gently encouraging. Usually, the quieter and more easy-to-overlook the information you receive is, the more you can trust it.

If you feel highly charged emotions when you receive your guidance, that's probably not your intuition. Instead, it's likely to be a reflexive reaction to past trauma that you've been through.

Your body stores the memory of any trauma you've experienced. Then, whenever you encounter a situation that reminds you of that first traumatic experience, your body goes into protection mode – sending out alarm signals that the new situation isn't safe. This can hold you back from trying new experiences and stretching beyond your comfort zone.

If, on the other hand, the guidance you receive involves negative messages about yourself or someone else, it's your inner critic. The same is true if the 'guidance' feels like you're being told off.

And either way, whether it's your trauma or your inner critic speaking, you don't need to listen.

Identifying your intuition when it speaks

To differentiate what's your intuition and what isn't, you need to get to know yourself really well.

Doing this starts with learning to regulate your nervous system, which can be as simple as giving yourself a moment to take a breath.

When you feel something that might be your intuition, notice the sensation you feel. Where do you feel it in your body? How emotionally charged does it (and do you) feel?

If you feel charged, take a couple of slow, deep breaths and exhale fully. Then, simply witness whatever's going on for you. Get present in your body, and let yourself breathe through the feeling.

Close your eyes, put your hand on your heart and remind yourself that you're safe.

How do you feel now?

Keep a record

Another important tool to help you differentiate your intuition from other voices is a record of how your past intuitive nudges have played out.

Start to keep a record of every internal nudge or feeling that you think might be your intuition communicating with you.

Note down how the message felt, where you felt it in your body and whether it was accompanied by any emotion.

Also note down anything that happened when you listened to the possible intuitive message. If you took action based on it, what was the outcome?

Keeping this kind of record will help you to clearly understand how stored trauma, fear and your actual intuition each feel in your body. As a result, you'll learn to untangle the voices of each and clearly know which one you're listening to.

Let your intuition come to you

Our culture doesn't teach us to listen to our intuitions. Instead, it teaches us to dismiss intuitive messages in various ways, for example...

- We can doubt ourselves by overthinking a situation and listening to other people's (many) opinions.

- Unconscious biasses, assumptions and judgements can drown out our intuitive wisdom.

- 'Should's and expectations can make us not want to 'cause a fuss', disappoint others or let them down.

- The desire for an opportunity, person or status can be bigger and louder than our intuitive voices.

- Previous trauma can disconnect us from our own experiences, leaving us distrusting ourselves and our intuitions.

Many years ago, someone asked outdoor survival expert Ray Mears how to get the most out of their upcoming trip to the jungle.

His response has always stayed with me. He said, and I'm paraphrasing, "Walk into the jungle and stop. Let the jungle come to you."

Wow! I just love that for soooo many reasons.

I mean, of course... it's obvious. If you go stomping through the jungle, all the creatures you're there to see will run away from you. You won't notice any of the incredible diversity that surrounds you.

But how often have you wanted to ask your intuition something, then been so 'noisy' that you scared off any signs and synchronicities before you noticed them?

You need to stop and let your intuition come to you.

However, stopping is easier said than done in today's world. Life is constantly getting busier and faster and noisier. Technology has made life so much easier and more accessible, but it's also added a different level of stress and a constant ability to be 'on'.

With many people now working from home, the boundaries between 'working' and 'not working' time and space have become increasingly blurred. As the meme I saw the other day put it: "We're not working from home. We're sleeping at work!"

It's now more important than ever to disconnect from the noise around us and reconnect to ourselves so we can get in touch with our intuitions and trust ourselves.

And the practices you'll learn in this book will help you to do just that.

Energetic Hygiene

You're stumbling through energetic smog

Every day, you're in contact with people and the world.

You interact with family, friends, colleagues, acquaintances and neighbours. You scroll through social media, watch the news and learn what's going on politically. Perhaps you'll experience conflict, or have uncomfortable conversations with others. You may have arguments or disagreements.

Regardless, every time someone comes and 'offloads' all their angst on you, you take it on in your energetic system. The same thing happens when they share their fears and concerns or ask your advice, or when you witness or experience a trauma or tragedy.

Additionally, we're all constantly surrounded by judgements, negative opinions, disempowering thoughts, media and advertising, movies, shows and social media. And of course, most of us own all kinds of devices that encourage us to scroll excessively.

On top of all this, the world bombards us with messages about who we should be, what we should do, how we should spend our time and what we should achieve and accomplish.

Together, all of these interactions and experiences immerse us in an 'energetic smog' of other people's thoughts, feelings, fears, judgements and opinions.

And that smog can make it impossible to clearly see what belongs to you and what belongs to other people. This, in turn, can leave you uncertain about what you really want, and what you are and aren't comfortable doing to make it happen.

I'm sure you've experienced the feeling of having a great day until someone who isn't comes along, and all they want to do is moan. Then, after they leave, you just feel drained.

Or you watch a film, and even though you know it's just a story, you still find yourself crying or angry at the injustice one of the characters experiences. Many years ago, I watched *Into the Wild*, which had such a sad ending that I physically felt 'off' for hours after the film finished.

This happens because every time we interact with someone or something – even if it's fictional – we exchange energy with it, creating an energetic connection.

Some of those connections are tiny, with very little emotional charge. Perhaps someone held the door open for you and you said, "Thank you."

The energetic 'cord' from this kind of exchange would be less than the thickness of a single hair, and would naturally dissolve as the day went on. You might not even remember it a couple of days later.

But some energetic connections are far more substantial, and create a higher emotional charge. For example, if you've had a major disagreement with someone, the energetic exchange and the resulting connection will be much more significant.

Think of *these* energetic cords as massive data cables that send and receive information between you and the person you're connected to.

Now, this kind of cord can be a positive thing. If someone loves and supports you, you can receive that love and support through your connection with them. However, the opposite is also true: people can project their fears and judgements along the cord, and you can pick up on them.

Some of the things you might notice if you're experiencing this kind of unsupportive energetic exchange include:

- doubting yourself
- making a decision and then changing your mind
- feeling like you're taking three steps forwards and then stumbling two steps back

The answer: better energetic hygiene

Back when I first started my kinesiology training in 1999, the tutor recommended a particular Psychic Protection class. The teacher for that class described picking up on other people's energy in this way:

"Imagine you're a farmer who's been out in the fields and mucking out the animals all day. When you come home in your muddy boots and dirty overalls, do you sit on the couch straight away? Of course not – that would be

> ridiculous! It would leave mud and muck all over your home, so it just doesn't make sense. And your energetic health is the same way, except that you don't see the mud."

I wasn't really into the idea of 'psychic' anything at the time, but I went along to the class anyway. And that training was probably some of the most valuable of my life because it started my interest in – and research into – energetic hygiene.

And gradually, as I learnt more about the topic, I became more aware of how other people interacted with my energy, and how I used my own energy with them. I grew more conscious about how I interacted with others, and started to take responsibility for how I showed up – not only in life, but in relationships too. I also learnt to take responsibility for my past decisions and actions, and take greater responsibility for my choices moving forward.

If I felt drained or depleted around certain people, I gradually learnt how to clear those feelings, and come back into my own energy. And with time, I even stopped allowing others to drain or deplete my energy. Instead, I began to quickly recognise that depletion was imminent, and 'protect' my energy by setting boundaries.

Learning about energetic hygiene taught me to understand where my energy ended in the world, and where other people's began. Whenever I noticed an intense emotion, I could quickly distinguish whether it was mine, or if I was picking it up from someone else or the collective energy around me.

And the techniques I learnt worked! Even after 20+ years of working energetically with thousands of clients, I never pick up anyone else's 'stuff' now, much less keep it with me.

Now, don't get me wrong. I'm highly intuitive, and have many 'clairs' (my word for a finely tuned sense that goes beyond the physical – think clairvoyance for clear-seeing, or clairaudience for clear-hearing). And I can still use my clairs appropriately when I want to.

But I always *choose* when, where and how I use these skills, which means they never overwhelm me.

Another part of avoiding overwhelm is routinely using the practices I mentioned in the Introduction to keep my energy running clear and free. These practices also help me to make powerful choices about overcoming obstacles that come my way. Plus, they help me to discern the times I need to lean into a setback and keep going from the times I need to turn around and take a different path.

And best of all? They help me to feel clearer about any decisions I need to make.

So let's dive into the practices themselves, beginning with the one I try to start my morning off with as often as possible... the SACRED practice.

Practice One:
The SACRED Practice

The SACRED Practice Overview

As we started to talk about in the Introduction, the SACRED practice helps you to get clear on what you want to do and how you want to show up in the world.

It gives you a moment to connect with your body and to become present. It also helps you to make choices from a place of clarity and feeling centred, rather than one of fear or overwhelm.

And all of those outcomes make it the perfect practice to start your day.

SACRED is an acronym (I love acronyms!) made up of the first letters of each step. These are:

- **STRIP** off all of your jewellery and crystals, so you can feel YOU. Feel how your energy flows naturally, and notice where your 'edges' are.

- **ALIGN** your energy, using simple practices to remove anything that isn't yours or that no longer serves you. Bring yourself back to your centre and connect with your own truth.

- **CONNECT** with your Higher Self, your inner-most knowing, to receive any messages it might have for you (and help you to trust anything you receive).

- **ROOT** into your true essence, so that you're grounded and present.

- **ENCIRCLE** yourself with your energetic shield, supporting your boundaries to keep out whatever isn't yours and protect whatever is.

- **DECIDE** what you want to experience during the coming day / week / month, and then draw that to you with powerful, aligned intentions.

In this section of the book, I'll guide you through each of these steps in the SACRED practice in detail. Keep in mind, however, that what I show you is just a template. I want you to make the practice your own.

So, as I walk you through each step, I'll also give you ideas to help you create your own practice. Use your intuition and creativity to experiment with different options and discover what works best for you.

First though, let's talk about what makes the SACRED practice so helpful.

Why the SACRED practice is important

I created the SACRED practice by combining some of the practices I routinely used to keep myself – and my energy – feeling good. Over time, I refined them into the step-by-step practice you'll discover in this section. Following it will help you to let go of all the energetic 'dirt' and baggage you've accumulated, leaving you feeling lighter, fresher and more deeply connected to yourself.

As I mentioned in the previous chapter, this helps you to step out of the energy of overwhelm. Then, when you have to make a decision, you know you can trust your choice to be right for you. You can make it from your own energy, free from other people's judgements, expectations and influence.

This is essential, because if you make your decision based on what your family, your culture or society in general expects, you'll likely end up frustrated, bitter or resentful. Deep down, you'll know it wasn't the option you really wanted... so chances are that you won't take action to follow through with it.

But if you decide based on what's most aligned for you, you're much more likely to see the decision through. Making your decision this way helps you to navigate any obstacles you encounter with more ease because you're more confident in your choices.

The SACRED practice gives you this alignment and confidence by helping you to identify which energies, thoughts, fears and emotions are genuinely yours. That means you can also tell which belong to the people, culture and society around you – in other words, it helps you to cut through the noise of everything that *isn't* yours.

As a result, you can easily clear your energy of all the judgements, expectations and energetic grime that you've picked up from others.

It's a bit like taking an energetic shower.

Think about it: we wash our bodies, brush our teeth and clean our clothes because we recognise that dirt and muck build up on them. Imagine wearing the same clothes every day for a month, and not washing for that whole time. By the end of the month, you'd feel fairly grotty, right?

The SACRED practice will do for your energetic system (and therefore your ability to make good decisions) what taking a shower and changing your clothes will do for your body. It will leave you feeling vibrant, refreshed, clear and confident.

And, while you're at it, the practice will also help you to untangle what's yours from what's not, ensuring you're ready to enjoy whatever the coming day brings.

Step 1: STRIP

The first step of the SACRED practice is to strip off any crystals or jewellery you're wearing.

We often wear crystals and jewellery (and clothes and other accessories) to generate certain feelings, or to energise or recharge us. In other words, we wear them to change and influence our energy.

That isn't helpful during the SACRED practice, because the practice is about understanding and connecting with your own energy. In the practice, you explore how your natural, unassisted energy feels and flows. That way, you can quickly identify when external energy is influencing you, which then allows you to confidently declare, "Actually, that's not mine."

Once you've identified the external influence, you can ground back into your own wisdom, moving forward and making any choices from a place of clarity. You can know that you're aligned with your own values and Higher Self, rather than reacting from fear, judgement or not wanting to let other people down or disappoint them.

So, just for this practice, take anything that changes your energy – including jewellery and crystals – off. You can put them all straight back on afterwards.

(Note: when I'm walking people through this practice, I'll often joke that they should strip off their clothes too. That isn't necessary, but you might find it interesting to try the practice naked and notice how your energy feels when you're completely free.)

Once you've removed everything, get ready to feel into your natural energy.

The Practice: Stripping and feeling into your own energy

After taking off your crystals and jewellery, take a moment to feel into your body.

> What do you feel?
>
> What sensations do you notice?

Next, feel into the quality of energy within your body.

> Is it light and flowing freely, or does it feel tired and sluggish?
>
> Sometimes, it may feel heavy. Sometimes, it'll feel great. And some days, it'll feel somewhere in between.

Finally, feel into your energy field (around your physical body, extending out about an arm's width).

Stretch your arms horizontally out to the side to get an idea of how big your energy field is.

Can you feel the edges of the field? Do they crisply, clearly define your space? Or are they a bit wobbly? Perhaps you can't feel anything at all?

Be gentle with yourself as you begin this practice.

Notice what you notice. Don't get distracted by emotions, feelings or judgements about it. Just be a curious observer.

If you find yourself wanting to label things as 'good' or 'bad', try replacing those thoughts with, "Oh, that's interesting!" or, "Hmm, I hadn't noticed that before."

Approach this step with an open heart. Aim to be expansive, playful and curious. Imagine you're going on a fun adventure to learn more about someone you really love and want to support through life. Because that's exactly what you're doing, and that person is *you*.

Remember that there's no right or wrong way to feel. You're just observing, witnessing and collecting data.

It's all just valuable information.

If you struggle to feel energy...

Try this practice if you're struggling to feel into your energy – and especially the energy around you.

Hold your hands about 1m apart from each other, with your palms facing inwards.

Close your eyes and notice whether you can feel anything.

Move your hands a little closer, then stop for a few moments to see whether you become aware of your energy. You might feel that energy as a pulse, as a small magnetic pull or as heat or tingling in your hands and fingers.

If you don't feel anything, move your hands a little closer again, then stop and check again.

Keep moving them closer and stopping, and see when you become aware of your energy.

Whenever you notice it, make a note of what you feel.

Then stop and rest.

Shake your hands gently with your fingers loose to reset the energy in your hands.

Next, repeat the exercise. But this time, when your hands are about 20cm apart, hold them there.

Imagine you're now holding a ball of energy between your hands.

Feel the ball getting stronger and stronger, and the energy becoming more powerful.

After a minute or so of doing this, bring in your breath.

On the inhale, feel the energy in your hands become stronger.

On the exhale, feel the energy leaving your hands.

When you can clearly feel the energy, start to move your hands back and forth. See if you can feel the energy change as your hands move.

If you push your hands closer together, does the energy feel denser?

As you pull your hands further apart, can you feel the energy stretch?

Again, write down whatever you notice.

When you're comfortable with that exercise, hold the ball of energy in your hands once more. This time, practise telling it what to do.

Keep your hands 20cm apart, and this time, tell your energy to feel heavier and denser.

Next, tell it to move to your left hand and then to your right.

Practise directing your energy with your intention.

And again, write down your experiences and whatever you notice.

Finally, when you've finished the exercise, place your hands over your stomach and feel yourself re-absorbing your energy.

Shake your hands with your fingers loose to reset and clear any excess energy.

Practise this regularly to deepen your connection with your own energy.

'Stripping' helps you to use crystals more effectively

When you practise this step regularly, you'll get used to feeling your own natural energy. After you've done that, you can bring the crystals and the jewellery back in, and see what changes you notice once you're wearing them.

You've probably read books or articles that tell you things like, "citrine is for abundance and joy," or, "obsidian is protective." But we're all individuals, and different crystals can affect different people in different ways.

The wonderful thing about this part of the SACRED practice is that it helps you to understand how each crystal affects *your* individual energy. Once you know that, you can choose the most effective stone for you in any given moment, rather than choosing based on a generic description.

For example, you might discover on a given day that rose quartz energises you, even though its 'book' meaning is all about love and relationships. So you'll be able to say, "Oh, I feel a bit flat today – I'd better wear my rose quartz when I go out."

The 'book' description may have recommended, for example, carnelian to increase your fire energy and creativity. But maybe your energy was actually flat that day because you needed to show yourself some love and compassion? If so, wearing carnelian might have over-sensitised you and left you feeling wired and jangly – a bit like crystal caffeine!

The practice of first stripping all your crystals off will help you to 'learn yourself' intimately. That knowledge then gives you the confidence to choose the most nourishing, nurturing, supporting crystal for you in that moment.

Key insights to take with you

- Stripping off your crystals and jewellery helps you to get a sense of how your natural, unassisted energy feels.

- Without doing this, it's hard to tell what's your own energy, and what's part of the energetic fog of outside influences you're walking around in.

- As an added benefit, getting familiar with your natural energy helps you to use crystals more effectively when you want to change it to something else.

A question to think about...

How DOES your natural energy usually feel when you remove anything that influences it?

Step 2: ALIGN

The next step in the SACRED practice is to align.

Aligning means bringing your energy back into harmony with your core essence. This frees you from any of the energetic debris that you've accumulated from external sources.

Aligning is all about new beginnings – fresh starts, confidence, optimism, hope and trusting yourself deeply. It's about bringing yourself back into alignment with who you are, with your truth and with your own centre.

This step is so important because – as we discussed in the Energetic Hygiene chapter – every day, we're bombarded with other people's energy, thoughts, feelings, judgements and expectations. As I said previously, it's like walking around in an energetic smog.

Taking the time to regularly come back into alignment with yourself helps you to clear away anything that you identified in the previous step as 'not yours'.

I like to see this as a way to create breathing space for yourself by pushing away everything that *isn't* you. So instead of anxiety, confusion or overwhelm, you'll experience a moment of calm where you feel centred and grounded.

It's a space where you can collect your thoughts, feel what's really true for you and realign with what's important to you.

How to align your energy

There are so many ways to create that energy alignment.

Find a simple, quick method that works for you. Use whatever feels right at the time – on different days, you may want to use different techniques.

I've listed out some suggestions to try below, or you might have a different tool or technique that you already know works for you. Regardless, I'd recommend trying as many as you can, because each technique will change your energy in a different way.

You might find that one technique works best for you when you feel tired and sluggish. Another might be more beneficial when you're overwhelmed, and a different one altogether might work when you feel joyful.

Experiment with the ideas below and find what works best for you at different times. Then simply do whatever most helps you to feel aligned and centred on a given day.

Align using smell

I love working with scents because they have such a deep body connection for me. Every time I smell my burning rosemary and lavender bundles, my body reacts instantly. It's like my energy knows exactly what to do to snap right back into alignment.

To create different scents, try:

- **Herbs or incense**: Burn the dried herb or incense and carefully waft the smoke through your energy field. I do mean 'carefully', though – I have plenty of holes in my clothes and carpet to prove I need to be more careful when I'm burning things!

- **Essential oils**: Try using a diffuser and waft the mist around your energy field, or make a spray and mist it around your body. Alternatively, add a few drops of a skin-safe oil to a carrier oil, rub it on your hands and then move them through your energy field. Imagine that you're brushing your energy body with the oil from the top of your head to the bottoms of your feet.

No matter what scent you use, the basic principle is the same. Sweep the aroma all around you throughout your energy body (just a few centimetres away from your physical body this time). This removes the layers of energetic debris, mud or smog, refreshes your energy and brings you back into alignment.

Align using sound

Sound is another powerful tool to work with, as it gives you very clear, immediate feedback. Some options to try include:

- clapping
- cymbals
- drumming
- finger clicks
- rattles
- singing bowls
- tuning forks
- voiced sounds, eg. song, chants or prayer

Whatever sound you make, really listen to its quality. Does it resonate clearly, or does it feel dull?

As you move the sound around your body and through your energy field, does it sound the same everywhere? Are there areas where it seems to stop short or sound duller?

If so, pay more attention to those areas, as the energy there may be stuck, dense or 'dirty'.

Keep using your sound until its quality resonates beautifully (or at least better than it did before) all around you.

Align using crystals

Crystals are another fun way to align your energy, and my personal favourite is selenite.

I have a selenite log that's about 30cm long and 3cm wide. It honestly feels like a lightsaber as I swish it around my body. I may have even been known to make lightsaber noises as I do this (obviously, they're optional!) I also like to use a polished oval piece of selenite, which I run through my energy field like a bar of soap.

The nice thing about selenite is that you don't have to cleanse it – plus it's fairly inexpensive. Don't submerge it in water, though, as it can dissolve!

Of course, you can use any crystal that calls to you, or that you have to hand. If you already have them, some options you might want to try include:

- black tourmaline
- carnelian
- citrine
- clear quartz
- rose quartz
- selenite (obviously)
- smoky quartz

Whatever crystals you use, move them through your energy field in a way that feels right for you. You could try my lightsaber or bar-of-soap movements above, or experiment and find something that works better for you.

Align using movement

You don't actually need any tools to align your energy. You can simply move your body.

Here are a few ideas for specific movements:

- dance
- flick your limbs
- shimmy and shake
- stomp your feet
- rub or massage your skin
- tap your fingers

Perhaps you could use your hands to brush energy off around your body. Or you could kick your legs and flick your arms to release energy from them. Another option is tapping your fingers all over your body. Yet another is cupping your hands and gently making contact with your body. (Although if you do this, the emphasis is on being gentle. You're looking to move your energy, not bruise yourself!)

Whichever option you try, move with the intention of breaking up unwanted energy and getting rid of anything that doesn't serve you.

Other ways to align

Finally, you can realign your energy without any tools or movement at all. Here are three of my favourite ways:

- **Breathwork**: Close your eyes to block out all external stimuli, then place your hand over your heart to connect deeply with your body. Focus on your breath, then breathe in deeply for a count of six and exhale fully for another count of six.

- **Nature**: Doing the breathwork practice above outside and connecting to nature will realign your energy and help you to find your own natural rhythms.

- **Water**: You could also make the practice of aligning a part of your physical morning routine. At the end of your shower or bath, spend a few moments visualising the water washing away the energy that isn't yours down the plughole and into the drain.

All of that said, coming back into alignment might just be as simple as taking a deep breath.

It might be sitting down with your feet flat on the floor, walking in nature or looking at the sky.

It could be literally anything. So explore. Experiment with all the different options available to you and see what works best for you.

Practise, and then practise again

Whatever you choose to do to align, you'll need to practise it over and over again. Gradually, the repetition will begin to create an immediate alignment response within you.

For example, you could choose to combine looking at the sky with taking a single deep, centred breath. Then you could tell yourself, "Every time I look at the sky and breathe deeply, that'll bring me back into my own body. It'll bring me back into alignment with myself."

Eventually, once you've repeated the association enough, you'll create an automatic cue for your body. Then, every time you look at the sky and take a deep breath – whether consciously or not – your body will know, "Oh, this is when we come back into alignment."

Plus, the more often you practise, the sooner you'll recognise when you're out of alignment. And the more you practise with different tools, the more quickly you'll know exactly what you need when you're anything but aligned and clear.

The Practice: Aligning your energy

Whichever technique or tool I choose from the options above, I like to align using the following sequence:

I start the process by clearing unwanted energy from above my head to free up the connection with my Higher Self. This ensures that I can connect with my deepest knowing and inner-most wisdom.

Then I move down to my throat to remove anything that's preventing me from speaking or expressing my truth.

Next, I move to the area around my ears to help me clearly hear my intuition.

After that, I clear the area over my shoulders to release any responsibilities I've picked up that aren't mine to carry.

Then, it's down my arms and around my hands. I clear my dominant hand first, so I can let go of what no longer serves me, then my non-dominant hand to receive what I want and need.

Next, I move down the midline of my body. As I do, I pay attention to any part of me that calls for my attention through a twinge or a thought to move it.

After that, I move to the area around my hips and energetic womb space. (This is the abdominal area in which some people have a physical womb, but that's not necessary. You might also know this area as the Sacral

Chakra or Hara – regardless, it's an energetic place of darkness, nourishment and creation.) Here, I clear away anything that prevents me from accessing my ability to create – whether I want to create art, words or a loving home.

Then, it's down around my legs, so I can confidently walk forward on my path.

And finally, I focus on the area under my feet to help me take a stand for what's important to me.

Try using this sequence as a starting place, but – as with everything else in this book – feel free to change it however you like to suit you.

Lastly, before you finish with this step, take a moment to notice how your energy feels right now. Is it different compared with how it was at the beginning of the Align step?

If so, what's changed? Are you more aware of your energy? Are you starting to notice your energetic edges more clearly?

Or perhaps you haven't noticed anything at all?

Again, there's no right answer. Just remain curious and open as you move on to the next step.

Key insights to take with you

- Aligning releases any of the energy you've taken on from other people or outside situations once you've identified it.

- Until you align with what's yours and let go of everything that isn't, you'll feel buffeted around by the winds of other people's expectations and judgements.

- There are many ways to realign your energy, and different techniques will work better in different situations – so try as many as possible.

- Over time, repeating a technique again and again will create an immediate alignment response in your body, making it quick and easy to align with your core essence.

A question to think about...

Which techniques work best to align your energy in which situations?

Step 3: CONNECT

The next step of the SACRED practice is to Connect.

The world can sometimes feel overwhelming. Many of my clients say that since they've stepped out onto their own paths in life, they sometimes feel alone. They feel like the people around them don't understand their choices, or that they now experience the world in a very different way from their friends and family.

This part of the practice reminds you that you're not alone. You're part of something much bigger, regardless of your personal beliefs.

And when you take a moment to step back and acknowledge that you're part of something greater, your perspective changes.

Think about it. We really are incredibly small. We're each just a tiny little speck of dust on an amazing planet, spinning within its own solar system. And that solar system, in turn, moves within its own galaxy, which is again within its own universe.

I don't say this to take away from the real issues we face as people, communities or societies. I say it because taking a moment to step back and feel the spaciousness around you gives you the ability to breathe. It lets you know that, no matter how you feel in *this* moment, there's more than enough room for you and your biggest feelings and emotions.

It also reassures you that you're allowed to take up space. It helps you to realise that you don't have to keep everything inside. You don't have to do everything alone.

When you connect to something bigger than yourself, you begin to remember your connection to your highest knowing and your deepest wisdom. You tap into the infinite energy that gives you the inspiration – the nudge – to remind you that you're not alone.

And it only takes a couple of moments to feel that thread of connection.

Accessing cosmic intelligence

As you practice connecting, you begin to become aware of an infinite cosmic intelligence that lies within and around you. Turning inwards lets you connect with this cosmic intelligence. When you do, you realise that it's somehow both bigger than you – filling entire universes – and within you at the same time.

As within, so without.

This cosmic intelligence isn't something you can rationalise or intellectualise. You can only experience it. Its depth and expansiveness make it hard to define with words. It shifts, changes and merges with all that is.

And as you connect with this intelligence, you open yourself up to another world. It's a world governed by mystical laws that you can use to bring deeper connection and understanding into your own life.

You'll hear the cosmic intelligence speak to you through the language of your soul and your intuition.

Remember how we said in the Intuition chapter that your intuition provides immediate information that bypasses your conscious thoughts and rational mind? Well, your intuition doesn't create its conclusions by weaving together stories or learnt knowledge. Instead, it offers information direct from that cosmic intelligence, via your soul.

This information will keep you safe and reveal the truth of a situation. It may even inspire you towards a life where you can express your Highest Self and fullest potential.

The Practice: Connecting to the cosmic intelligence

To connect to the cosmic intelligence, first close your eyes and put your hand over your heart space. This is the area of your energetic body that's just above the centre of your chest. It doesn't map exactly to the location of your physical heart, but it feels like your emotional centre.

Visualise a beautiful silver energy filling up your heart space and the whole of your chest.

Let the silver energy nourish, restore and revitalise you.

Once your heart space is full, take some of that silver energy and send it up to the heavens in a silver thread – perhaps to Father Sky, your soul star or your soul family.

It doesn't matter what you believe in. What matters is that you're sending this energy up to connect with something 'bigger' than you are.

When I do this part of the practice, I like to think of the silver thread as being like the string of a musical instrument. I want my thread to be lovely and taut, just like an instrument string – not slack and wobbly, or out of tune.

That way, any notes, messages, guidance or communications that pass along it flow freely and easily, and are clear and resonant.

Spend some time feeling this connection. If you have a question about your life or next step, this is the moment to send the question 'up your silver thread' so your highest wisdom can send the answer back down for you to receive.

Your answer might come immediately, or it might come later as a flash of inspiration over the next few days.

Either way, you'll get the answer you need to hear.

Key insights to take with you

- Connecting with a higher, deeper cosmic intelligence helps to release the sense of loneliness that many people feel when they step onto their own path.

- Additionally, connecting with this intelligence allows you to hear the voice of your intuition more clearly.

- Your intuition is a valuable source of guidance and wisdom, but unless you actively give it a channel to speak through, you may not hear its voice.

A question to think about...

What imagery best helps you to connect with your inner-most wisdom and intuition?

Step 4: ROOT

The next step of the SACRED practice is to root, which means grounding yourself so that you feel safe in your own body.

Grounding doesn't always sound very sexy or exciting. Let's face it – floating off to other realms to get inspiration and intuition in the Connect step seems like *much* more fun.

But we need to ground ourselves to actually manifest all the inspiration, dreams and ideas we receive within the physical world. Being grounded and rooted allows you to show up in the world with presence, power, certainty and clarity.

In fact, being grounded is the only way to begin consciously creating the life, communities and world that you want. Yes, you'll get ideas and inspiration for your goals and desires when you're connected to your Higher Self. But the real magic can only happen when you bring that energy back down and root it into the Earth.

That's why bringing the energy of your imagination, dreams and inspiration into reality requires you to root that energy (and yourself). Only then can the things you want manifest in a way you can physically experience. Only then can they become tangible in this world so you can actually have them.

And the only way to make *that* happen is by grounding yourself here on Earth.

Think about a tree.

Many trees – especially trees like oaks – grow phenomenally high. When you look at a massive tree, though, you don't see its root system, which is often twice as big as its canopy. After all, the bigger and stronger a root system, the more it can hold above the ground. If a mighty oak has an enormous canopy and tiny little roots, one strong breeze could bring it crashing down.

Rooting creates strong foundations for the tree. That way, when storms and winds come or people climb it, it can remain standing strong and tall in its space. It can continue to grow and support everything that it looks after – its fruits and acorns, its squirrels and badgers and foxes, and everything else in its ecosystem.

So, although you can't generally see a tree's roots, they're just as important (if not more so) as everything you see above the ground.

And it's the same for you. You *also* need deep roots to be able to support yourself, your own ecosystem, and all of the different things that are important to you. You need strong, sturdy roots to stay grounded when you weather your own storms.

Rooting yourself and your energy gives you a solid grounding – a strong foundation. Just like the tree, the deeper you sink your roots, the stronger and more secure you'll be. Then you'll be able to reach further and create more.

When you send your roots down, know that you're rooting into your own wisdom. You're rooting into your strength, your power and the power of the Earth.

In much the same way as you reached upward to Father Sky in the Connect step, you now sink your roots down to allow Mother Earth to hold you. Nothing is expected of you. You don't need to ask permission to do anything. You can simply *be* here, where you belong, with the unconditional love of Mother Earth holding you.

Know that you can relax completely into this energy of being held, supported and nourished.

Know that you're safe.

And remember that your roots need to be bigger and stronger than everything else you do.

It's hard to make a clear decision without roots

The lack of roots is most obvious to me in people who need to make a big decision.

Let's say you need to decide on something important. Your initial decision feels clear and inspired... right up until you share it with well-meaning friends and family, who immediately say things like:

"Are you sure?"

"Why would you want to do that?"

"How do you know that will work?"

And then you start to doubt yourself.

You wonder if you're good enough. You backtrack on your decision and then think, "Oh, maybe I shouldn't." Perhaps you feel let down and disappointed.

And then you have to decide all over again.

When you can root into your own energy and truth, though, your inner wisdom will help you to bypass the whole self-doubt, self-criticism and 'Should I / shouldn't I?' energy.

Instead, you'll be more like the tree. You'll stand tall, firm and true, knowing that you've made the right decision for you, regardless of what other people think or say.

The Practice: Rooting into the Earth

To root yourself and your energy, close your eyes and place your hands over your energetic womb space.

Visualise this space – and your entire pelvic girdle – filling with a beautiful golden energy.

Let the energy flow around this sacred area, gently releasing anything within you that no longer serves you, and activating whatever needs to be activated.

Then, when you feel good, send some of this golden energy down into the Earth, just like tree roots.

Feel these roots going down into the centre of the Earth, then spreading out to the side to make you feel really safe, stable and held.

Imagine them travelling downward through an underground stream.

Let the cool, refreshing mineral water of this stream wash away any patterns or behaviours that aren't yours, that you've outgrown or that no longer serve you.

When you start to feel lighter and cleansed, let this energy travel up through the rest of your energy system, so that your whole body experiences the refreshment.

Next, allow your roots to travel even deeper towards the centre of the Earth, this time passing through crystal caverns.

Notice what crystals are there to support you. You might know each crystal's name, or you may just see a colour, or experience a feeling.

Regardless, let yourself receive nourishment from these crystal allies, feeling their energy travelling up your roots and into the rest of your system.

Once you feel ready, send your golden roots down even further until they reach a beautiful golden ball of energy right in the centre of the Earth.

Allow them to wrap around this ball of energy and become one with it.

Know that the Earth is holding you. Know that you're safe, protected and nourished.

Spend some time really allowing yourself to experience this energy. Again, nothing is expected of you. You have nothing to do and there's nothing to prove.

Just surrender into the energy of being safe and held.

Finally, when you're ready, come back to your physical body. Know that you can access this energy of grounded centredness anytime throughout the day.

No matter what comes your way or how buffeted by life's experiences you may feel, you can always reconnect with your roots to feel grounded and anchored once more.

And again, before you move to the next step, check in and see how your energy feels different compared with the beginning of the practice.

What's changed?

Are you more aware of your energy?

Perhaps you're starting to notice how you feel within your own body?

Maybe you feel more present and grounded?

Regardless, notice any changes.

Key insights to take with you

- Rooting means grounding yourself, your energy and any ideas and inspirations you've received into the Earth.

- It may not seem 'sexy', but it's essential if you want to bring those ideas and inspirations into reality and manifest them in the physical world.

- Much like a tree, your energetic root system needs to be big enough to support everything else you want to do and create in your life.

A question to think about...

What imagery best helps you to ground yourself and root deep into the Earth?

Step 5: ENCIRCLE

The fifth step of the SACRED practice is to encircle your energy system with clear boundaries.

When your boundaries are strong, clear and backed with the power of your presence, other people can recognise and honour them.

So in this step, you'll encircle your energy system with a beautiful purple bubble. You don't have to be able to feel, see or smell this bubble. The important thing is just to set the intention and then know that it's there.

I recommend using purple because it taps into the Violet Flame of transmutation. So if anything comes your way that doesn't serve you, the bubble simply transmutes it for the highest good of all involved. No drama – it's just gone. And anything that *is* yours and does serve you just comes straight through the bubble, cleansed and cleared to nourish and support you.

I often think of the purple bubble as an energetic immune system. It creates a clear boundary – a barrier between what's yours and what's not. It allows in nourishment, and keeps out anything that may cause you harm or discomfort.

It's a bit like breathing too, in that you don't need to think about your purple bubble for it to work. When you bring your attention to it, though, it becomes much more effective.

This powerful practice helps you to feel safe and establish strong, tangible boundaries. That's essential, because as your energetic boundaries become stronger, your personal boundaries in life strengthen too. You start making those boundaries a priority, and you quickly notice when something or someone compromises them.

You get clearer on what you will and won't accept, and you get more confident about speaking up when you need to.

Perhaps you feel more comfortable telling someone that their behaviour around you isn't okay. Maybe you confidently say, "No," to something that you don't want to do. Or you might start setting limits – both with yourself and other people – around your resources.

Plus, when life gets too busy and everything feels like it's 'too close' and overwhelming, it's hard to think clearly. Forming your purple bubble creates space around you, making it easier to step back slightly from everything. This gives you the sense of being able to breathe more easily and get a clearer perspective on the overwhelm.

That space then allows you to say, "Oh my goodness! That thought, that belief, that doubt in myself – that's not mine! That's actually somebody else's!" Maybe it's your mum being overprotective. Perhaps it's your culture expecting you to follow this career path. Or perhaps it's society telling you that you have to follow this route in life to be successful...

Regardless, that space helps you to clearly identify which thoughts and feelings are yours, and which you're absorbing or are being projected onto you.

That clarity then makes it easier to know what you need to do next. If whatever comes up is yours, you can address it. If not, you can remind yourself that it doesn't belong to you, and set it down again.

As you practise visualising your bubble, you may want to change aspects of it. Here are a few things to think about playing with.

What size is your bubble?

Your purple bubble probably won't be static. Just like a real bubble, it will change and move – shifting size and moving gently around you.

Visualising your bubble isn't about creating an iron shield to hide behind and block all of life out. It's about connecting with the energy of a living, breathing bubble, and allowing it to communicate with you and to respond to what you need.

Some days, you might want your bubble super snug and close to you, to keep you feeling safe and cosy. On other days, that closeness might feel claustrophobic and restrictive. On those days, you'll want it expansive so that you too can feel expansive.

Your bubble size might also depend on where you're planning to be. I live in the countryside, so I'm used to having a lot of physical space around me. When I go into the city, I keep my bubble quite close to me because I don't want everyone walking through it.

As you go through your day, you might find your bubble's size needs to change too. You might start off with a really big, expansive bubble, then want to pull it in closer to you throughout the day. Or the opposite could be true.

Keep playing around with different sizes for your bubble to find out what works for you in each situation.

What texture does it have?

I love the softness and playfulness of a real-life bubble, but you can create different textures for your energetic bubble depending on what you need at a given time.

For example, if you're about to have a difficult conversation or you feel a little uneasy about an upcoming event, you might want to feel a bit more protected.

In these situations, I like to imagine adding a layer of flexible purple paint to the outside of my bubble with a paintbrush or a roller brush. I set the intention of covering my whole body, including the areas that often get neglected like the soles of my feet, my back and the top of my head.

But, as with all parts of the SACRED practice, do whatever works for you. Someone once said, "Rebecca, I'm using a cement mixer today." That imagery always makes me chuckle!

Some days, you might need really thick boundaries. On those days, get out your trowel and clearly define your edges as you go out into the world.

Does it have any other colours?

You can also play with adding colours to your bubble. If you're feeling a bit low in energy, try putting a layer of red around the outside of your purple bubble. Then take a moment to notice whether the red makes you feel energised and ready to go… or if it's so intense that it makes you uncomfortable.

If the red doesn't feel good, imagine washing it off and replacing it with orange. Maybe that makes you feel joyful and a bit more positive?

Keep playing with different colours to see how each one makes you feel.

When you know what works for you, you might call in different colours for different days. For example:

- Traditionally, red is energising, but that might not always be true for you.
- Some shades of green might feel peaceful, while others might feel quite icky.
- Blue might feel calming or too cold.
- Dark navy is a very protective colour for me, and it can help me to feel invisible on the days I don't want to be seen.
- Maybe some days you'll want a rainbow or polka dots or green tartan.

Be open and curious as you explore how you feel when your bubble is 'wearing' different colours. Eventually, you'll know exactly which colour you need the moment you wake up and feel a particular way.

But regardless of the colour you use for your layer, always start with a basic bubble of purple for protection and to tap into that energy of transmutation.

The Practice: Encircling your energy with a purple bubble

Start by imagining yourself surrounded by a beautiful, shiny, purple bubble.

Imagine this bubble being light and moveable, just like a real bubble.

Feel yourself safe and centred within it.

Remember that your energy system typically extends out to an arm's width away from your body, and start feeling your purple bubble around its edges.

Notice how your energy feels with the bubble around it.

Next, try changing the size of your bubble.

First, in your mind's eye, imagine pulling your purple bubble closer to you.

How does that feel? Is it better or more restrictive?

Next, imagine pushing your purple bubble out much wider, as far as you can imagine.

How does that feel? Does it feel expansive or overly vulnerable?

Play around with your bubble, until it feels great to you.

Lastly, you might want to 'customise' your bubble.

> If it feels right to, imagine changing the texture of the bubble around you, and see how it feels.
>
> Or alternatively, imagine adding a layer of paint, in any thickness you want, being sure to cover all areas of your bubble.
>
> Take a moment to really savour your own energy within this clearly defined space that you've created.

As you practise visualising your purple bubble more, you'll start to notice when other people's energy tries to enter your space and unduly influence you over the day.

When this happens, you'll be ready and prepared to respond to it, rather than reacting.

You'll also feel calmer because you're responding from a place of presence and clarity, rather than feeling overwhelmed by the events and people around you.

Key insights to take with you

- Encircling means surrounding yourself with a bubble of protective energy to keep what's yours in, and what's not yours out.

- Visualising this energy as a purple bubble will draw on the transformational power of the Violet Flame.

- You can experiment with the size, texture and additional colours of your bubble according to the situation at any given time.

A question to think about...

What types of bubble work best for you in which situations?

Step 6: DECIDE

We've reached the last step of the SACRED practice: Deciding.

In this step, you'll decide how you want to experience your coming day (or week or month), and then lock that decision in with a power pose.

This is the place of your magic.

It's time to decide

When you reach this stage of the SACRED practice, you're in the perfect place to manifest exactly what you desire.

Your energy is flowing clearly, you're connected to your Higher Self and you're rooted into your truth. In this moment, you're not influenced by anyone else's judgements, expectations or desires.

You're ready to direct your energy wherever you choose.

You might decide to manifest something really tangible. Maybe there's something on your to-do list you want to finish, or a conversation that you know you need to have.

You could also decide to experience more of your values and your core desired feelings, and bring those front and centre in your life.

Regardless, decide what your intention will be, then feel into those core feelings, values, experiences or events. Imagine what you'll feel like once you've had that difficult conversation, or ticked that item off your to-do list.

Imagine and feel into these things as if they've already happened. Your body and mind don't understand the difference between reality and imagination. So just feel your intention as if it had already happened. As you do this, you're saying to the Universe, "Thank you. More of this, please."

You can feel or picture the outcome you decide on in any way you want.

Maybe you feel your desire as a colour around you. Perhaps you see it as a crystal or a flower, or a sign over your chest. The details don't matter. There's no right or wrong way to do this, as long as you're connecting with and feeling into the experience.

Lock your decision in by taking up space

Then, once you've fully felt into whatever you've decided on, lock it in with a power pose.

Power poses are stances or gestures that let you take up space. You can see this 'in the wild' when runners throw their arms up in the air as they cross the finish line. You can also see it when someone pumps their fist skyward in celebration after achieving something important to them.

According to research from Amy Cuddy, power poses also reduce the stress hormone cortisol and increase your confidence on a physical level. (Amy has a fabulous TED Talk on power poses that I recommend checking out to fully understand their value.)

Mentally, striking a power pose reminds you to take up space with your thoughts, feelings, dreams, decisions and physicality. And from an energetic point of view, power poses expand your energy field, which again, creates space for you to think, feel and dream.

You may not be aware of how ingrained being 'small' is in our culture, and how it keeps you from taking up space and expressing yourself fully. But for too long, people – in particular, women – have been told that they're 'too much'. They're too loud, too emotional, too high-maintenance, too… something.

Society constantly tells us that our value lies in being small – both physically and behaviourally. In fact, we're regularly judged by our body size: the smaller we are, the more acceptable and worthy we are. Why else would the weight loss and diet industry be worth $192.2 billion in 2019 and be growing quickly, according to Allied Market Research?

But being small goes beyond body size. Women are told to 'act ladylike', which usually involves being meek, demure and undemanding. It means putting other people first, and staying quiet about anything that inconveniences others or makes them feel uncomfortable.

It means not causing a fuss.

So, right now, I want you to take up space. Take up ALL of the space around you. Make yourself as big as you physically can, and notice how it makes you feel.

Give yourself permission to keep on physically taking up space.

Doing this locks in the intention you decided on by also allowing your decision to energetically take up space.

The Practice: Deciding on your intention and locking it in

Now that you've completed the first five steps, you're in the perfect place to decide on your intention/s for the coming day.

Your energy is running free, clear and uninterrupted by the noise and busyness of life. So what do you actually want now?

Trust that your energy is in the perfect state to tell you what's best for you.

If you don't have a specific decision to make, close your eyes, put your hands on your body, and ask what the best use of your time and energy is.

Will you focus on an activity, or on experiencing more of your values?

Maybe you want to start – or stop – doing something?

Perhaps you need to reach out to someone for support?

This isn't about trying to do everything, but you do need to decide what you want to achieve with all your newly aligned energy.

Then, once you've decided, spend a few moments really feeling into the energy of your choice, as if it had already happened.

Finally, when that feels good, move into a power pose.

Try raising your hands above your head and out to the side, or place your hands on your hips.

(When I hold my hands above my head, it feels like I'm funnelling all the energy of my decision down to me. When I put my hands on my hips, I feel as if I'm making a statement to the world – something like, "You'd better believe this is happening!")

Stand with your feet further apart than your hips and allow yourself to take up space.

Some people I know do this pose in bed and call it their 'Starfish' pose.

If you have any mobility issues, just imagine yourself holding the power pose – you'll still experience the benefits.

Try out different poses to see how each feels for you. If they feel different, you may decide to use each one for a different kind of decision.

Hold your pose for as long as feels right to you.

> I set a phone timer for two minutes, which seems like a great amount of time to experience the pose's benefits for me.
>
> Try experimenting and hold the pose for more or less time to see what works for you.

When your timer goes off, you've completed the SACRED practice.

Let yourself smile, and move about your day feeling centred, grounded and aligned with what you want to create.

Key insights to take with you

- Once you've completed the first five steps, your energy is in the perfect place for you to manifest what you want next.

- Decide how you'll focus your newly aligned energy, and feel into the outcome of that decision.

- Finally, lock in the feeling and power of your intention by holding a power pose for as long as feels right for you.

A question to think about...

Which power pose feels most aligned for you in which situations?

After the SACRED Practice

Finally, after you've completed all six steps of the SACRED practice, notice how you're feeling.

Hopefully, you feel more aligned, connected or rooted. My clients also often describe feeling more grounded, lighter or more energised.

Or maybe you feel nothing right now.

Whatever you feel, know that it's perfectly fine. Just because you can't see something doesn't mean it's not real.

So don't worry if you don't feel the way you think you should. Remember that this is a practice. It will get easier and you'll create more tangible results every time you do it.

Remember too that a practice doesn't have to be long and complicated to be useful. You can do this entire practice in a few minutes. So even on the busiest of days, you can fit it in.

Just add it into whatever routine you already have, and it'll become something that you just do – much like brushing your teeth.

You'll find that once you do it consistently, you'll feel more aligned and on purpose. You'll make clearer, more conscious choices that support you in getting to where you want to go in your life.

Better yet, you'll be able to make a decision and stick to it. No more doubt, overwhelm or going back and forth with 'should I / shouldn't I?' conversations with yourself.

To get even more benefit from the practice...

To really get to know your energy intimately, and understand what affects and supports it, I'd recommend keeping a simple journal.

Every time you do the SACRED practice, make a note of how you felt before you started, and how you feel at the end.

Pay particular attention to whatever tools you used in the Align step.

Then at the end of each week, take a moment to reflect. Consider:

- how the quality of your energy changed from day to day
- how you honoured your needs and desires
- how you navigated any potential obstacles

Did you feel more aligned, fulfilled and on purpose on some days compared to others?

Perhaps other people's moods and experiences affected you less?

Maybe you could be more present for yourself and your friends and family?

People often tell me that they feel great when they do the practice, but that they didn't realise its true benefit until they stopped doing it. Suddenly, they found themselves starting to doubt and second-guess themselves again, and didn't know why.

Remember that – just like going to the gym – doing this practice once a week will have *some* benefits. But the more often you prioritise your energetic health and hygiene, the stronger your 'energy muscles' will become, and the clearer your energy – and life – will flow.

If you'd like to join me and follow the practice in 'real-time', visit www.RebeccaAnuwen.com/DecisionBonuses to access my videos.

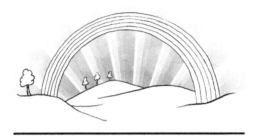

Practice Two:
The GRACE Practice

The GRACE Practice Overview

I've mentioned that I like to do the SACRED practice at the start of the day to align my energy and help me make clear choices that serve me throughout the day.

I like to do the GRACE practice at the end of the day or week to reset my energy and get me ready for a fresh start. This practice helps me to find energetic closure and reconnects me to my own energy. Beyond that, it reminds me to appreciate and celebrate myself, no matter what kind of day or week I've had.

Perhaps most importantly, the GRACE practice gives me a moment to reconnect to my priorities. It fills me back up with my own essence – literally helping me to become 'full of myself' again, regardless of how depleted I've become. (See the Call Back your Energy chapter for more about the importance of being full of yourself.)

GRACE – yes, it's another acronym! – stands for:

- **GROUND** your energy and become present to bring closure to the energy of the day or week, and get ready to confidently move forward.

- **RECOGNISE** all that you've done, achieved and consciously chosen not to do during the day or week, and savour your accomplishments so you can build on them.

- **APPRECIATE** yourself and take time to really honour who you are and how you've shown up in the world over the past day or week.

- **CALL BACK YOUR ENERGY** from external people, events or situations, so that you can move forward without letting the past influence your thoughts and decisions.

- **EMBODY** your truth, and become so full of your dreams and desires that you leave no room for other people's expectations and judgements.

Just as with the SACRED practice, in this section, I'll guide you through each step of the GRACE practice. But again, what I show you here is just a template, and I want you to make it your own.

So once again, use your intuition and creativity to discover what works best for you.

Why the GRACE practice is important

At the end of the day or week, it's so easy to focus on everything you haven't done or completed, or all the things you could've done better.

Most of us barely take a moment to recognise all that we HAVE done and achieved.

I know people who've published books, received a promotion or accomplished something that they've dreamed of for a long time. But instead of taking the time to enjoy and appreciate what they've achieved, they just move straight onto the next thing.

When we don't take the time to close out our day or week, we go into the next one energetically 'hungover'. The GRACE practice gives you a moment to reflect on everything you've done and let go of anything you haven't.

This helps to reset and refill your energy, so you're ready to start the next day or week refreshed and renewed.

Let's work through the GRACE practice step-by-step.

Step 1: GROUND

The first step of the GRACE practice is to ground your energy and become present.

If you're like many women, you spend a lot of your day focussing on what you need to do, and what's coming up in the future. Perhaps you feel nervous or excited about an event. Maybe you've already planned out what you want to happen.

But these events or achievements haven't actually happened yet – they're still in the future. You can't know exactly how they'll go, yet you spend a lot of time and mental space holding the energy of 'what if…' in your conscious mind.

Additionally, you probably spend yet more time going over and over past events. Maybe you regret a past action or inaction. Or perhaps you try to make sense of why something went the way it did.

Devoting so much mental energy to the past and future leaves you very little time to actually be in the present moment. And when your energy is also ungrounded, you can find it difficult to connect with how you truly feel, or what you want or need in this present moment.

As a result, you may feel like you don't have a foundation – that you're floating outside or alongside your body. You may find yourself in your head more, and have difficulty connecting to your heart and your intuition.

You can also find yourself feeling scattered, distracted, powerless and unsafe, unsure of what to do or think next. Excess energies from anxiety or overwhelm can crackle and buzz through your system like lightning, and if you don't ground them, they can leave you feeling 'fried' and at your wits' end.

So, much as a lightning rod on your home diverts and grounds electrical energy in a thunderstorm, you need to be able to ground any excess energy you're carrying. This allows you to neutrally witness and observe events, and review the situations in your life without the energy of judgement.

Grounding your energy also allows you to energetically return to your body and truly receive the nourishing steps in the rest of this GRACE practice.

The Practice: Ground

Start the GRACE practice by taking a moment to ground yourself into the present moment.

The quickest way to ground your energy is to close your eyes, and then...

Put your hand over your heart space.

Take a couple of deep, centring breaths.

When you close your eyes, you shut out the distractions of the world around you. Closing off your visual sense heightens all your other senses, helping you to become more aware of how you're feeling in the moment.

Placing your hand over your heart space connects you with your body. It moves you out of your mind, helping you to step away from logic and reason and connect more deeply with your feelings.

Focussing on your breath then gives you something tangible to pay attention to. It connects you with your own internal rhythm of breathing: in and out, in and out.

Breathing slowly and deliberately is one of the most effective ways to calm your nervous system, bringing you a sense of peace and well-being.

Breathe in deeply.

Exhale fully. This is your time to just be in this moment.

Don't think about what's happened during the day (that comes next) or start planning for tomorrow. This is your moment to just become present with yourself.

Breathe in deeply.

Exhale fully.

Notice how you feel as your energy begins to calm down and return to your body.

What's changed?

Do you feel calmer, or more aware of your feelings?

Perhaps feeling your feelings is a new experience. It might be uncomfortable to start with, so be gentle with yourself if so.

Either way, remain curious and open to the possibilities available to you when you feel safe in your own body.

Other ways to ground your energy

Focussing on your breath isn't the only possible way to ground your energy. Experiment with some of the following options and see if any of them ground you more effectively than the breath focus.

Indoors

If you're doing your GRACE practice indoors, try one or more of the following options:

- Use the Rooting exercise from the SACRED Practice section.
- Sit with your feet flat on the floor and feel the connection with the energy of the Earth below you.
- Massage or rub your physical body to help you become aware of it.
- Dance or stomp your feet.
- Drum – and the deeper the sound of the drum, the better.
- Make deep, guttural noises with your voice.
- Place a rock, stone or pebble by your feet.
- Place a piece of bloodstone or red jasper by your feet.
- Wear red socks – yes, really!

Outdoors

If you're doing your GRACE practice outdoors, you can also try one of these options:

- Walk around barefoot in the grass, sand or even mud.
- Lie with your back flat on the Earth.
- Paddle in the ocean.
- Notice and become present to the weather elements around you.
- Stand with your back against a tree (hugging it is optional!)

Key insights to take with you

- Grounding into the present moment is essential to channel and divert all the excess energy you've picked up over the day or week.
- Much like a lightning rod diverts the powerful electrical energy of a storm, grounding diverts the energies of anxiety and worry so they can't distract or overwhelm you.
- One of the simplest, most powerful practices to ground your energy is to focus on breathing slowly, deeply and fully.

A question to think about...

Which of the grounding techniques above resonate best with you in which situations?

Step 2: RECOGNISE

The next step of the GRACE practice is to recognise yourself.

The world we live in values doing and achieving above everything else. Success is too often measured by what you've done and achieved, not by what you've contributed.

So, at the end of the day or week, if you still have tasks left on your to-do list, they become the focus. All the things you *have* ticked off just fall by the wayside.

Perhaps you've accomplished something really significant. You might have completed a course, got a new job or achieved a long-held goal. But instead of taking the time to really savour your triumph, you just move straight on to the next thing on your list.

Of course, accomplishments don't always have to look like 'doing something major'. Sometimes, the biggest achievements are about consciously choosing NOT to do something – saying "No," to an opportunity or prioritising your rest.

Society doesn't see these types of accomplishments as worth recognising, but they're important to acknowledge as steps towards your own measure of success. This kind of recognition – without judging yourself for whatever you haven't completed

– does more than just make you feel good. It also allows you to build on your successes, helping you to achieve more of what's important to you over time.

And finally, recognising yourself is important because identifying everything that you've done gives you a sense of identity as a unique individual. It's easy to lose this sense of yourself, especially if you've been through a major life event such as getting married or divorced, having a baby, changing job or retiring.

Recognising yourself helps you to remember everything you do as a person, and everything you contribute to your own life and the lives of those around you.

Recognise ALL your different accomplishments

Once you feel grounded and present in this moment, allow yourself to recognise all that you've done and achieved throughout your day. Trust me: there'll be more of it than you think.

I like to split 'recognising' into four sections.

Section 1: What big things have you achieved?

First, think about the significant things that you've accomplished. This could include:

- major items that you've checked off your to-do list
- tasks or projects that have taken a lot of your time, energy or resources
- activities that have pushed you out of your comfort zone

For example, maybe you've had to have a difficult conversation or enforce your boundaries.

Maybe you've completed that task you'd been postponing for months.

Perhaps you've received a pay rise or been offered a new job.

Maybe you said, "No," to someone and prioritised your own needs instead.

Whatever these major accomplishments might be, recognise them first.

Section 2: What everyday tasks did you do?

Next, think of all the small, habitual 'adulting' tasks you need to do each day. You might not give much thought to these tasks because they're so routine.

But while these jobs may be quick and easy and require little thought, they still take time and energy to complete.

If you're not sure what to include here, start by thinking about self-care activities, for example:

- washing and other personal hygiene tasks
- ensuring you have clean clothes to wear
- grocery shopping and preparing meals so you have food to eat
- moving your body
- staying hydrated
- taking your vitamins
- arranging health appointments
- going to bed early or taking a nap

Also think about looking after the home you live in. This might include:

- cleaning and tidying so that your house is a comfortable place to live
- putting bins out so that your rubbish gets collected
- paying your utility (and other) bills on time

Finally, look at tasks you do to keep your life running smoothly, for example:

- keeping your car fuelled up
- returning library books before they're due
- managing your money
- making sure you get to work on time
- getting your children to school on time with their homework completed

Scan back through all the daily tasks that you do. Individually, each one may not feel very 'significant', but they all add up. Plus, you've still done that task rather than doing something else, so recognise that you've chosen to get it done.

Section 3: How did you support other people?

Next, think about all the ways that you've helped and supported other people. This might include:

- supporting friends, family, community members or even complete strangers
- giving your time or resources to others – perhaps helping a friend, or donating to charity

- offering a kind word or encouraging someone to make a change
- helping someone with a new hobby
- listening to someone who needed to talk
- giving advice when someone asked you for guidance

No matter what the details were, allow yourself to recognise how you showed up for others.

Section 4: How did other people help you?

Finally, think about how other people have shown up for you. Ask yourself:

- How have other people supported you with their time, energy and resources?
- Who showed up for you?
- Who was there when you wanted a friend?
- Who's encouraged you or given you a helping hand?

This *seems* to be about what other people have done, so you may wonder what it has to do with recognising yourself.

The answer is that other people can't show up for you unless you first create and nurture relationships with them. So it's important to recognise the role you've played in creating those relationships, without which people couldn't support you.

The Practice: Recognising yourself

Place your hand over your heart and run through each of the sections above, one by one.

> As you do, really allow yourself to savour all that you recognise about yourself.
>
> Let your recognition encompass all you've done – from the small, everyday adulting tasks, to the actions that have stretched you and made you grow.
>
> Also, recognise all the ways in which you've taken a stand for yourself and made time to do what's important to you (which could also mean choosing *not* to do something).

Remember that recognition isn't just about achieving and doing – it's also about being and brewing. As we'll talk about more in the Sacred Pause practice, a pause is every bit as important as an action.

You may want to start a journal that documents all that you recognise about yourself.

Then, whenever you feel that you're not where you 'should' be, or that you'll never complete your to-do list, take a moment to read through all of the things you've already done!

You'll soon be feeling inspired by yourself.

Key insights to take with you

- Because our society values achievement over all else, it's common to ignore everything you *have* accomplished and focus on everything you haven't.

- Recognising yourself reminds you of all the things you've achieved, which can help you to build on them – and also strengthen your sense of identity.

- It's important to recognise not just the 'big accomplishments', but also the small, routine tasks and the things you've chosen NOT to do.

A question to think about...

Which accomplishments feel easiest and most natural to recognise yourself for, and which feel like they 'shouldn't count'?

Step 3: APPRECIATE

The next step in the GRACE practice is to appreciate yourself.

After you've spent some time recognising all that you've done for yourself and others, you'll hopefully be starting to fill up with good feelings about yourself.

Now I want you to take this to the next level, and really appreciate yourself for who you *are*.

This is about building on the energy of recognition to recognise and admire your inherent good qualities – above and beyond what you've done. You've probably practised appreciating other people, opportunities and situations you find yourself in. (And if not, that can be a really positive practice too.)

Just for this practice, though, I want you to focus on appreciating YOU.

It's far too easy to judge yourself, compare yourself to others and measure your achievements by someone else's ideas of success. That's even truer in the world of social media, where it's easy to confuse the unedited mess of your 'real life' with the filtered highlight reel of someone else's life.

This kind of judgement makes it easy to slip into patterns of self-criticism. To step you out of the energy of comparison and wanting, it's important to appreciate yourself just as you are.

The Appreciate step helps you to break those disempowering patterns and replace them with kindness, self-compassion and dare I say it... self-love.

We're all messy, complicated, paradoxical humans with our own sets of quirks. In fact, those quirks are what make us wonderful, unique and worthy of appreciation.

So take the time to really appreciate yourself and all you do. As you do this:

- Appreciate your unique values and way of seeing the world.

- Appreciate the way you approach life – it may not be perfect, but whose version of perfect are you comparing it to?

- Appreciate your body – again, you may feel it's not perfect – but again, whose version of perfect is your baseline? If parts of your body don't work well or are in pain, try to recognise the parts that are healthy. Don't try to pretend that your body's perfect as it is, but show it some much-needed love and compassion anyway.

- Try to even recognise how fabulous you are at your less-than-helpful habits (like noticing every single mistake you make), while at the same time, working to upgrade those habits.

Appreciation helps you to love and approve of yourself, and stops you from looking for external validation or trying to live up to other people's standards and expectations.

The Practice: Appreciating yourself

Take another deep breath and ask yourself what you can appreciate about yourself today. Perhaps it might be:

- the joy and humour you bring to your own day, and to other people around you

- your skill at baking your favourite cake

- your ability to take a stand for yourself or something that's important to you

- your willingness to choose something that you don't enjoy now, because you know your future self will thank you for it

- the benefit you enjoyed today because you were willing to choose what was right for you in the past, instead of taking the easy option

- the pleasure you experience from simply wearing your favourite clothes

Whatever you identify to appreciate about yourself, allow yourself to savour the appreciation. Spend some time feeling awe about who you are and everything that makes you YOU.

Once again, you may want to write down all that you appreciate about yourself in your journal to brighten your day whenever you feel 'less than'.

Other ways to appreciate yourself

Sometimes, taking tangible action can help to boost your sense of appreciation for yourself. Try:

- letting yourself receive other people's appreciation by writing down all the appreciative acts or words they offer you
- writing down at least three things that you appreciate about yourself each day
- repeating affirmations that carry the energy of appreciation (see below for ideas)
- saying, "Thank you!" to yourself for any reason (or no reason at all)
- doing something kind for yourself
- taking yourself out on a date or buying yourself a gift
- giving yourself something you want, now – no need to wait
- being your true self at all times

Affirmations

Affirmations are simple statements that describe an outcome you want in the present tense, and which you repeat regularly.

They're a powerful way to change your negative self-talk into something more positive and supportive. I've listed some suggestions below, but affirmations are far more powerful if you create your own.

You can use any wording you like for an affirmation, but there are three 'rules':

- **It needs to be phrased positively**. Describe what you *do* want, not what you don't: "I love and accept myself" rather than "I've stopped hating myself".

- **It needs to be phrased in the present tense**. Describe the outcome as though it's already happening: "I love and accept myself" rather than, "I want to love and accept myself".

- **It needs to be believable for you right now**. If your mind immediately sneers, "Yeah right, whatever, who are you kidding?", you're just affirming the dismissal. Try to find a baby step on the way to your outcome that you can believe in: "I am open to loving and accepting myself" instead of "I completely love and accept myself".

A few affirmations that you can experiment with include:

- I love and accept myself completely.
- I am more than enough.
- I am perfect just as I am.
- I choose myself.
- I believe in myself.
- I am healthy and happy.

I recommend saying your chosen affirmation(s) at least once every morning, and then ideally regularly throughout your day.

You can repeat them in the shower, sing them as you make your breakfast or record them and listen to them as you walk, run or drive.

For an extra dose of magic, repeat them while looking yourself in the eye in the mirror. This may be uncomfortable to start with, but the more you appreciate yourself, the easier and more enjoyable the experience becomes.

I call affirmations 'vitamins for your soul'. You might not notice any benefit immediately, but if you use them daily, the benefits compound and you start to enjoy their results.

Key insights to take with you

- Appreciating yourself builds on the energy of recognition in the previous step, and also helps to counter negative self-talk.

- It's important to appreciate yourself not just for everything you've done, but also for everything that makes you the unique person you are.

- Affirmations can be a powerful technique for helping you to appreciate yourself exactly as you are.

A question to think about...

Which qualities or characteristics feel easiest and most natural to appreciate yourself for, and which feel uncomfortable to acknowledge?

Step 4: CALL BACK YOUR ENERGY

The fourth step of the GRACE practice is to call back your energy.

As we discussed in the SACRED Practice section, every time you interact with someone, you create an energetic connection with them. Sometimes these connections can be useful, but often they just leave you confused and doubting yourself.

Calling back your energy fills you up with the energy that belongs to you. It makes you, quite literally 'full of yourself.' That's good, because when you're full of your own energy, there's no room for other people's. Nor is there any room for external judgements and expectations, which means you stay clear and aligned with what's true for you.

During this step of the GRACE practice, you'll consciously release any energetic connections you've made that don't serve you. Then you'll call back your energy from wherever you've 'left' it – in both cases, using your breath to release and reclaim.

Why you need to be 'full of yourself'

Here in the UK, saying that someone's 'full of themselves' is usually a criticism.

I have a very different take on the matter. As far as I'm concerned:

> ## YOU NEED TO BE FULL OF YOURSELF!

Now, when you read that sentence, you might find yourself reacting and judging me.

Of course you might.

Because, regardless of where you live now, you were probably encouraged to stay small from the time you were a young child. We talked about staying small physically back in the Decide chapter of the SACRED Practice section. On top of this, depending on where you grew up, you might have been told:

- not to get too big for your boots (in the UK)
- not to act above your station (in Ireland)
- not to get too big for your britches (in the US)
- not to be the tall poppy (in Australia or New Zealand)

No doubt every country has some kind of similar saying that encourages people to play small – to be accommodating and *selfless*.

'Selfless' – I really hate that word! People say it as if it's some kind of virtue... but really, why on earth would you celebrate not having a self?!

Surely it's the very act of being yourself – your whole self – that makes you the incredible person that you are? How can you be the fully self-expressed person you have the potential to be if you have no self to express?

Now, being 'full of yourself' doesn't mean becoming a horrible narcissist who never cares about anyone else. Nor does it mean that you think you're the ONLY one who deserves to have their needs met. But it *does* mean that you become discerning about meeting your own needs, and about how you choose to use your time, energy and resources.

Being full of your own energy also means you get used to prioritising your own needs over the expectations and comfort of other people. Of course, sometimes you'll compromise. Sometimes you *will* put others first, but when you do it, you'll do it consciously. It will be your choice as an exception, rather than the default expectation.

Another reason to be 'full of yourself' is that if you're not full of your own hopes and dreams, you leave empty space in your energetic body. And since nature abhors a vacuum... that space is where other people's energetic judgements and expectations will slip in.

I've been a kinesiologist for the last 20+ years, and worked with thousands of women over that time. And I've noticed that women who try to be 'selfless' almost never believe in or trust themselves. How can they, when they're trying so hard not to have a self to believe in or trust? With that loss of belief comes a disconnection from their dreams, desires and inner power.

This then muddies the waters of what they want for themselves. Their vision for their ideal life is blurred by everyone else's energy and desires.

So, even if it doesn't feel comfortable right now, you need to give yourself permission to become full of yourself. Give yourself permission to take up space with ALL of you: your thoughts, feelings, dreams, desires and physicality.

Of course, you probably won't become 'full of yourself' overnight. But you might gradually start to notice the places where you *aren't* full of your own hopes, dreams and desires – and that's a powerful start.

Once you notice the old stories and patterns, you can start to unravel them. You can begin to create space to re-write your own stories and consciously choose how you want to respond to life, rather than react. You can start to hear the voice of your intuition and make choices that are right for you, rather than ones that harm you.

The Practice: Calling back your energy

Start by visualising the same purple bubble around you that we talked about in the SACRED practice. Remember that this purple bubble taps you into the Violet Flame of transmutation. When you release energy that doesn't serve you, it passes through the Violet Flame, which cleanses and transforms the energy before it returns to where it belongs.

Once you've felt into your bubble, release anything from your energy system that isn't yours, or that doesn't serve you, by exhaling.

On each exhale, set the intention to release whatever no longer serves you.

As you exhale fully, feel your shoulders drop, your jaw relax, your teeth unclench and your eyebrows soften. Feel the energy around you become more spacious.

Know that you're releasing all the energetic connections you've created with people, places or events that don't serve you, whether you created them today, this week or years ago.

You may want to breathe out with slightly more force than normal, or just keep your breathing soft. Do what feels right for you in the moment.

Then allow your breath to flow naturally in again.

On your next breath, once again exhale fully, again feeling your body relax, release and become lighter.

Continue this for as long as feels comfortable and good – perhaps just for three breaths, or it may be more than ten.

When the releasing feels complete, you'll have made space within yourself that you can call back and receive your own energy into by inhaling. Again, as your energy returns to you, it passes through the Violet Flame, which cleanses and clears it for your highest good.

(Sidenote: this is a great practice to do by itself if you ever feel confused about what to do next. As you call back your energy, you'll feel lighter and clearer on your next step.)

First, take a few regular breaths to prepare yourself to call back your energy.

This time, breathe in deeply, right down into your belly. As you breathe in, feel your belly expand and set the intention for your energy to return to you.

Then let your breath flow naturally out again.

As you take your next deep breath in, feel your energy returning to you through time and space. You don't need to know where it was, just know that as it returns to you, it comes back through your purple bubble cleansed and clear for your highest good.

Feel yourself being filled up with your own energy and essence. Let yourself feel energised, refreshed and renewed.

Once you've completed this part of the practice, take a moment to simply notice how it feels to be in your own energy, and quite literally be full of yourself.

Notice how your energy feels different from the way it did at the beginning of the practice.

What's changed?

Are you more aware of your energy?

Perhaps you feel more energised, present or content?

Maybe you feel calm and at peace?

Notice any changes, and then move to the next step.

Key insights to take with you

- Calling back your energy helps you to become 'full of yourself', which is essential to become clear on your goals, dreams and desires, and then achieve them.

- Although we're taught to be 'selfless', this is an unhealthy state of being in which we don't know what we want, let alone allow ourselves to prioritise it.

- To become 'full of yourself', you need to release the energetic connections that don't serve you, and then call back your own energy from wherever it currently lies.

A question to think about...

How can you allow your own goals, desires and energy to take up more space within you?

Step 5: EMBODY

The final part of the GRACE practice is to embody the truth of who you are.

You've grounded your energy, recognised and appreciated yourself, and then called back your energy.

Now it's time to take a moment to remember and really savour the truth of who you are.

This is time you can just spend coming back into a loving, caring relationship with yourself.

It's a time to feel into the truth of who you are.

If you're not sure of who you are – if you've forgotten what's important to you or lost your sense of self – this is the perfect time to remember and reclaim yourself.

ALL of you.

Your thoughts, your feelings, your dreams, your desires, your quirks... all of it.

Remember that you do yourself and the world around you a great disservice when you only show up as a shadow of yourself.

Have you forgotten who you truly are?

It's all too easy to forget who we are and what's important to us – we just get caught up in the busyness of life.

Big events shape us, and we live out many roles, often prioritising everyone else's needs over our own (after all, we're supposed to be 'selfless'!)

We start to identify completely with a role – maybe as a daughter, a lover, a wife, a mother, a career woman, a divorcee, a retiree…. the list goes on. And each time we try to fit ourselves into the shape and expectation of the role, we lose a little more of our true essence.

Close relationships can be particularly difficult to navigate without losing your sense of self. The other person's needs can take centre stage, so you try your hardest to please them, regardless of your own feelings. Maybe you stop pursuing your own hobbies and interests as you prioritise the other person and their desires.

Over time, you can actually start to lose part of your identity.

If I do this, I just become 'Rebecca – Jamie's wife', or even worse, simply 'Jamie's wife'.

Or maybe my only identity is 'Solomon's mum'. Or 'Head of the Department'.

You might initially feel happy choosing to change your identity in this way. Or it might have happened without you noticing. Either way though, each time you identify yourself fully with a role, it can chip away a little bit more of your own unique sense of identity.

And that's in a fairly healthy relationship!

Unfortunately, many people are in relationships with family members, friends or a romantic partner that *aren't* healthy. In these relationships, the other person actively (whether consciously or not) undermines their relationship partner's sense of self.

Restoring a strong 'sense of self' allows you to embody your truth, which in turn helps you to remember who you are and what's important to you.

Knowing who you are and honouring this means being aware of – and respecting – your values, beliefs, personality, priorities, boundaries, emotions, habits, body and relationships.

It means really understanding your strengths and weaknesses without judgement. And it means being aware of all of your passions, dreams, desires, fears, quirks, likes and dislikes.

How do you like your eggs?

In the 1999 film *Runaway Bride*, Julia Roberts plays Maggie – a woman with a history of leaving men at the altar on her wedding day.

Ike (played by Richard Gere), interviews a string of Maggie's former fiancés, and one of the questions he asks them is how Maggie liked her eggs cooked.

Each man has a different response, but there's a common thread to their answers. One says, "Scrambled, just like me." Another replies, "Poached, just like me." A third says, "Fried, just like me."

In every situation, Maggie seemed to have liked her eggs exactly the same way as her partner did.

Later in the movie, Ike confronts Maggie, saying, "You were so lost, you didn't even know what kind of eggs you liked! With the priest, you wanted scrambled. With the deadhead, it was fried, with the other guy it was poached..."

Maggie tries to insist that she was just, "changing her mind," but Ike replies, "No, that's called not having a mind of your own."

So how do you like *your* eggs?

Questions to help you rediscover who you are

If you're ready to rediscover the truth of who you are, start by asking yourself:

- What values are important to you?
- What feelings do you want front and centre of your day?

Your honest answers will reveal who you truly are.

However, it's easy to choose what you think are the *right* answers, rather than the ones that are true for you. Sometimes, your true answers are buried so deeply under layers of expectations and conditioning that it can be hard to access them.

If that's the case for you, here are a few other questions. They may seem silly, but they're designed to bypass your logical, rational mind and dive deep into your truth.

For each of the questions below, write down the first answer that pops into your mind, even if it doesn't make sense. Trust that it's the right answer for you – if you overthink this exercise, it won't work.

- If you were an animal, what kind of animal would you be?
- If you were a flower, what type of flower would you be?
- If you were a colour, what colour would you be?
- If you were a biscuit (AKA a cookie if you're North American), what type would you be?
- If you were a season, what season would you be?
- If you were a pizza topping, what pizza topping would you be?
- If you were a tree, what kind of tree would you be?
- If you were a clothing item, what type of clothing would you be?
- If you were a piece of fruit, what kind of fruit would you be?
- If you were a book, what genre of book would you be?
- If you were a film, what genre of film would you be?
- If you were a restaurant, what kind of restaurant would you be?
- If you were a crystal, what kind of crystal would you be?

Now look at each of your answers and consider what it reflects about yourself. For each answer, ask yourself:

- how you feel about it
- what it reminds you of
- what it represents to you
- what memory you associate with it

Each answer will give you a little more insight into what's important to you.

You may even notice common themes coming up for you.

For example, if you thought of a lion and a sunflower for your first two answers, perhaps your theme is being braver and bolder? Or maybe it's taking up more space with your thoughts and ideas?

Or, if you thought of a dog and a dandelion, perhaps your theme is being loyal to yourself and valuing your dreams, even if the world rejects them as a 'weed'? (A dandelion is classed as a weed, but it's also a valuable herb with many medicinal benefits.)

The Practice: Embodying your truth

Once you have your answers to the questions above, spend some time really feeling into all of the things that are important to you.

Fill yourself up with the energy of your answers. Using the examples above, feel into what it would be like to be a lion or a sunflower.

Whatever the energy is, feel it filling you from the tips of your toes to the top of your head, down your arms and out your fingers.

Finish the practice by locking in this energy with a power pose, just as you finished the SACRED practice.

> Spend two minutes (or however long feels right) physically 'taking up space' in your pose, as you allow yourself to take up energetic space with the truth of who you are.

As you do this, smile.

> Smiling brings the energy of expansion.
>
> Smile as you give yourself permission to be full of your own unique essence.
>
> Then feel your true energy filling up your body and spreading through your entire energy system.

Give yourself a moment to enjoy just being you.

Other ways to embody your truth

Other techniques to embody your truth can include:

- asking for what you want, instead of prioritising other people's wants
- asking for something, even if you're not sure you want it, just because you can choose to do so
- spending time alone with yourself
- prioritising your own values
- making time for your hobbies and interests, or trying various activities to find out what you like
- trusting your energy and saying, "No," to what doesn't feel right, and, "Yes," to what does (even if you're scared of the "Yes"!)

- journaling about topics that are important to you
- thinking back to what you wanted to be as a child – for example, if you wanted to be an astronaut, maybe you value a sense of adventure?
- following your curiosity, and doing more of whatever you find interesting, without judging or needing to achieve anything with it

Key insights to take with you

- Your busy life, events, relationships and the roles you play can gradually chip away at your sense of yourself, leading you to forget who you truly are.

- Your sense of self includes not just what you are at your core, but also what you like and dislike, your interests, your passions and your values.

- Re-establishing that sense of your own identity is important because without it, you can't have a healthy relationship with yourself or prioritise what's important to you.

A question to think about...

What's the most effective technique for you to connect with and then embody the full truth of who you are?

After the GRACE Practice

The GRACE practice allows you to reflect on all that you've done, (or consciously not done) and achieved. It lets you truly recognise and find a deeper sense of appreciation for yourself.

This practice can bring you a sense of peace and closure – whether that's closure around people, events or just the week in general. As a result, it can free up your energy, allowing you to move forward with purpose and clarity. It effectively gives you an energetic reset to help you start the new day or week feeling complete, refreshed, calm and clear.

The GRACE practice also gives you the tools to make decisions from a place of deep connection to your own truth, energy and values. That means you can stop worrying about having to make the decision or sitting on the fence, unable to choose.

Instead, the practice gently dissolves the old energetic patterns and connections that have blocked you from making a clear choice. As it does, it helps you to become more 'full of yourself' – more confident in yourself and whatever decision you make.

As with the SACRED practice, after you've completed the GRACE practice, notice how you're feeling.

Maybe you feel more satisfied and connected to who you are?

Or perhaps you feel more spacious and refreshed?

As always, know that whatever you feel, it's perfectly fine.

And just like with the SACRED practice, don't worry if you don't feel the way you think you should. Again, it's a practice that will get easier every time you do it.

However you feel, aim to make the GRACE practice a part of your regular routine. You can do it at the end of the day, the end of the week or the end of the month – it's entirely up to you. Once you're doing it regularly, you'll feel a deeper sense of accomplishment, satisfaction and confidence in who you are and what's important to you.

Just as with the SACRED practice, doing it once a week will have benefits. But again, the more often you prioritise yourself and your energetic health, the stronger your 'energy muscles' will grow, and the clearer your energy – and life – will flow.

So again, I'd recommend keeping a simple journal of how you felt before the practice and how you feel afterwards. Note down too everything that you recognised and appreciated about yourself. This creates a beautiful journal that you can refer back to any time you need to remind yourself of how great you really are!

Finally, at the end of each week (or even each month), take a moment to reflect back and notice any changes in how you've been showing up for yourself and the quality of your relationships.

Perhaps you're speaking up for yourself or asking to have your needs met more?

Perhaps you've noticed other people dishonouring your boundaries and values – and instead of turning a blind eye, you've told them that you're not okay with it?

Maybe you've felt freer to choose what supports you and the life you want to lead, rather than feeling burdened by other people's expectations?

Whatever you notice, write it down – each change you notice over time will help to motivate and inspire you to keep doing the practice. And gradually, each change will help you make clearer, more confident decisions.

Again, if you'd like to follow along with the practice in 'real-time', visit www.RebeccaAnuwen.com/DecisionBonuses to access videos of the practice.

Practice Three:
The Sacred Pause

Why the Sacred Pause is Important

The SACRED and GRACE practices both include multiple steps. And while these steps are all quick and easy to do once you get used to them, sometimes you need to make a decision 'on the fly' – which often requires a simpler, more immediate practice.

When I need something to ground me and create space around me in the moment, I take a 'Sacred Pause'. I learnt this concept from Molly Remer, who in turn learnt it from Joanna Powell Colbert; and as soon as I heard the term, my body sighed 'yesssss' in relief.

I loved finding a phrase that matched the energy I knew I needed – the energy that's essential for every one of us.

In a world that values doing and achieving, giving yourself a moment to step back and honour the need for space can be hard. Yet the Sacred Pause is the very essence of life.

It's like walking a labyrinth

I like to think of the process of making a decision in the moment as being like walking a labyrinth.

When you enter a labyrinth, you do so with an intention. Often, you're seeking an answer to a question you hold in your heart.

As you spiral in, you let go of all the things that prevent you from finding the answer you seek.

Then, when you get to the centre, you pause. This moment of Sacred Pause is where you allow the answer to come to you. It's where inspiration occurs.

It's also where you assimilate whatever you receive.

Then when you're ready, you spiral back out of the labyrinth with clarity, having received the answer you sought. You're a new person who now has a choice to make: follow your guidance or reject it. Either option will change you and your experience of life, so you'll never be the same again.

And the Sacred Pause is quite literally at the heart of your experience as you decide which path you'll take.

Resting is as important as doing

I had this kind of experience with the Sacred Pause – although I didn't have a name for it then – when I started doing Kundalini Yoga.

I'd been dabbling with yoga for years, but I'd always focussed on doing it for fitness and flexibility. So when I started Kundalini Yoga, I was surprised to discover that we first held a pose and then rested for longer than we'd held it.

Initially, this frustrated me – I wanted to stretch and feel like I was 'doing' something.

But I chose to trust the process.

And I immediately noticed that during the pause – during that rest – I could feel my energy releasing and moving around my body.

That's when I started to value the importance of the rest, rather than just the doing.

I realised that within the rest, I made space for the magic to happen.

Ever since then, I've honoured the concept that the pause is just as important as the doing. I've understood that we need both. That's why, when I heard Molly Remer use the term 'Sacred Pause', my body immediately recognised it as a moment to give myself space. It was a moment where nothing was expected of me, and my only task was to allow myself to receive. In that space, I could receive rest, nourishment and the answers I sought to make my decisions.

I still tend to focus more on doing these days. But I also always ensure that I take at least one moment to pause and check in with myself each day.

I pause to integrate and allow life to come to me.

How to Take a Sacred Pause

One of the wonderful things about a Sacred Pause is that you can do it in a moment, even on the busiest of days.

In fact, the practice can create a moment to cut *through* that noise and busyness and allow you to become present.

The challenge is to remember that this tool is available to you.

It's to remember that whenever you feel overwhelmed, caught up in the energy of striving or anxious about the future, you can give yourself the gift of a Sacred Pause.

This steps you out of your current experience of life. It gives you the space to consciously change how you feel.

It's also a useful practice even when you're *not* feeling overwhelmed. For example, if you're caught up in routine, day-to-day activities such as working on your computer, cleaning or eating, the Sacred Pause creates a moment to check in with yourself.

It allows you to become present, notice how you're feeling and give your current task your full attention.

The Practice: Taking a Sacred Pause

The easiest way to take a Sacred Pause is to close your eyes and put your hand over your heart space, just like you did in the GRACE practice.

But this time, feel your body relax and let go of any thoughts or worries with every exhale.

Feel your shoulders drop, your jaw release, your teeth unclench and your eyebrows relax.

Feel your body and energy becoming softer.

You can do this in a few breaths.

As you do, notice how your body feels.

Can you allow yourself to pause, or do you feel your activity or your day calling you to resume it?

Try to give yourself this moment to compassionately witness what's going on for you with no judgement.

'Stacking' the pause

I'm a huge fan of 'stacking' your habits – adding new habits onto activities you already do.

In the GRACE practice, I mentioned doing your affirmations in the shower. That's a perfect example of habit stacking: you're already having a shower anyway, and you just 'stack' another activity on top of it. This saves you the effort of having to remember to do the second activity at a separate time.

Taking a Sacred Pause is a wonderful activity to stack on top of another daily habit you already have because you can do it anywhere, in any position. Regardless of whether you're standing up, sitting or lying down, you can take a moment to breathe and relax. That means:

- You can make your Sacred Pause the last thing you do before you get out of bed in the morning. Or you could make it the first thing you do after you lie down at night – or both.

- You can take a Sacred Pause after you get into your car and put on your seatbelt before you start each journey. And you can take another one when you arrive at your destination, after you turn off the engine but before you get out of the car.

- You can take a Sacred Pause before you start cooking your food, before you eat it and then again at the end of the meal.

- You can take a Sacred Pause at the beginning of a work task, and then again at the end. You can even take one at any time along the way when you feel tired, stuck or disconnected from the task.

There is literally no limit to the kinds of existing habits and activities you can stack a Sacred Pause on top of.

Other ways to take a Sacred Pause

As with each of the steps in the SACRED and GRACE practices, there are many ways to take a Sacred Pause. I've listed a few other suggestions below, but – as always – get creative and do whatever works for you. Remember that a practice can only work when you do it, so pick something you find simple and fun.

Like I said earlier, it doesn't matter which one you use, as long as you remember to use it.

It's worth practising each of the techniques you like to see which ones are the most effective for you in various situations. You'll likely find that you'll prefer one technique in one situation, and another in a different setting. You'll also probably discover a favourite technique that becomes your 'go-to Sacred Pause'.

It's a good idea to practise using each of the techniques that work for you at a time when you don't actually *need* a pause.

That way when you do need a Sacred Pause – when you're overwhelmed or have a decision to make – you'll already know how to best create the space you need. You won't need to spend time and energy figuring out which technique to use in that situation.

And that, in turn, means you'll have more resources available for your decision.

Here are a few other techniques to try.

Explore what you need

Sometimes, the simple act of asking yourself what it is that you need right now can bring you back into the moment.

Try placing your hand over your heart space to connect with your body, and asking yourself one of the following questions:

- What do I need right now?
- What can I give myself right now to feel fully satisfied?
- What do I need to make myself feel complete right now?

Notice that these questions focus on what you can do for yourself, not what you want others to do. They also avoid aiming for intensely 'positive' emotions like happiness or joy, which can be an unrealistic stretch and even *harmful* if they're not your authentic truth. This isn't about toxic positivity or emotional bypassing – it's about experiencing authentic presence and completion in the context of whatever's real for you right now.

Say your affirmations

As we explored in the GRACE practice, taking a moment to say your affirmations helps you to realign your energy.

Additional affirmations that you could try during a Sacred Pause include:

- I trust myself completely.
- I have more than enough time to complete my tasks.
- I find creative solutions to challenges I encounter.
- I am connected to my inner-most truth.
- I feel supported in every decision I make.
- With every inhale, I receive love and nourishment.

- I choose positive habits that support me.
- I prioritise myself and my needs with love and ease.

Strike a power pose

We used the power pose in both the SACRED and GRACE practices, but you can also use this technique on its own. You usually only need to hold a power pose for a few moments to lift your spirits and remind yourself of how capable you are.

I know many people who take themselves off to the bathroom to strike a power pose before an important interview or work meeting.

If you don't have much time, you can also start your day with a power pose, or strike one while you're in the shower!

Read your favourite quote or poem

A book of your favourite quotes and poems is a great tool for creating a Sacred Pause.

Simply grab your book, flick it open to a random page and allow yourself to be moved and inspired by your favourite writers.

You could even write your own words of wisdom to inspire yourself during your Sacred Pause moments.

Create a Book of Brilliance

Magical people often keep a Book of Shadows to record all of their magical workings. Alongside this, I recommend also creating a 'Book of Brilliance' that focusses on all the brilliance and joy you create and encounter as you move through your year.

To make your book, simply take a journal and – if you wish – decorate it in a way that feels great to you. Then add in pictures, quotes, poems, affirmations and experiences that add to the energy of living a brilliant magical life.

When you want to take a Sacred Pause, try reading back through your Book of Brilliance to remind yourself of the things you love that inspire you. Let the reminder bring you back to your centre.

Additionally, if you have to make a decision, spend a little time browsing back through your book to reconnect with what's important to you first. Then, once you're 'full of your own essence', make your decision from that space.

Drink a cup of tea or coffee

If you're like me, you love to have a hot drink at least once a day. (My brew of choice is nettle tea – I love it!)

The good news is that you can turn even something as mundane as your daily cuppa into a moment of Sacred Pause.

Once you've made your tea or coffee, sit down and drink it with intention. Breathe its aroma in deeply, then exhale again slowly.

Savour the taste, being present as you take each sip.

Notice its flavour, its fragrance, its temperature and even its texture.

Slow down and be present with yourself and the moment.

Of course, you don't need to specifically drink tea or coffee to do this. You could just as easily have a glass of cold water. All you need to do is slow down and become present as you drink.

That means no gulping or guzzling!

Use the power of visualisation

Again, tools can be useful to create a Sacred Pause, but you don't need them.

You can also simply close your eyes and imagine a place where you feel calm and rested.

Perhaps it's a place that holds happy memories for you. Or maybe it's somewhere you've never been, but would love to visit.

Either way, spend a few moments visualising that place.

Bring the visualisation to life as much as possible, incorporating all of your senses. Ask yourself:

- What can you see?

- What temperature is it? Can you feel a breeze, or the warmth of the sun on your skin?

- What can you hear around you? Is the sea lapping gently at the shore? Are people laughing? Is music playing or can you hear the rustle of a breeze through the trees?

- Notice what you can smell. Is there salty sea air, sun lotion, the sweetness of fresh fruit or the scent of damp, mossy forests?

- How do you feel emotionally in this place?

Get as much detail into your visualisation as possible, and allow this special place of yours to refresh and renew you.

Building a Sacred Pause into your routine

In much the same way as you can stack a Sacred Pause onto other regular daily activities, you can also build it into your spiritual routines and practices.

Add it to your daily devotional

If you have a daily spiritual practice, it most likely already has a moment of Sacred Pause within it. If not, you can easily add one.

For example, you can include a moment of inner reflection, meditation or prayer.

Or you can light a candle with the intention of bringing yourself clarity and calm.

Take a moment to explore which techniques would resonate best with your individual practice.

Use tools to tap into your intuition

We said back in the first section that tools aren't magical in and of themselves. You can, however, use them to tap into your own intuitive wisdom.

For example, you could draw a daily oracle card, charm or rune to seek guidance during your day. Before you do the draw, take a moment to breathe and feel your energy centre itself as you become more present.

Ask your question or just ask for general guidance, and then draw your selected item.

Spend a few moments reflecting on the message you've received.

You may want to note down your messages to look for themes as the days and weeks go by.

Try the Emotional Stress Release technique

One technique I learnt during my kinesiology training was Emotional Stress Release (ESR). In fact, on the very first day of our training, before the course had even begun, our tutor had us all do this exercise without telling us what we were doing.

She explained that she always did this to reduce the stress of starting something new, and it worked!

The exercise comes in two parts. The first part is great if you're short of time, or feeling light-headed or dizzy. The second part reduces stress and overwhelm.

You *can* do the first part on its own, but it's more powerful if you combine it with the second.

Part One

Before you start the practice, give yourself a score out of 10 for how you feel right now. Use a scale where '0' means 'cool as a cucumber', and '10' means 'the red mist has descended, and you can't think straight.'

Then tap on your chest in an anti-clockwise direction for about 30 seconds.

This will help to rebalance your energies.

Next, hold the reflex points on your head (see image below) and think about what's bothering you in as much detail as possible.

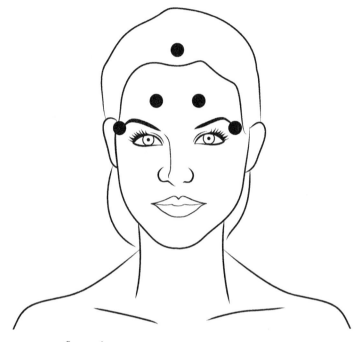

Image: reflex points

Think about who was there, what was said, what else happened and exactly how you felt. The more you feel as you remember this situation, the more energy you can release.

Then simply hold the reflex points for a couple of minutes.

When you're ready to stop, check how you're feeling again on the scale of 0 to 10.

You can hold the points for as long as you need to, but don't feel as though you have to keep going until you've hit 0. Sometimes, just moving a few points from an 8 to a 5 is enough to be able to continue without feeling consumed by anger.

Part Two

Hold the five reflex points from the image on the previous page:

- one point at either temple
- one point at each 'frontal eminence'
- one point at the anterior fontanelle

The easiest way to hold these points on yourself is to place:

- your thumbs on your temples
- your little fingers on your frontal eminences
- your index or middle finger on your anterior fontanelle.

Hold these points for a few minutes or until you start to feel calmer.

Key insights to take with you

- While the SACRED and GRACE practices are fairly short, sometimes you need something more spontaneous to recentre yourself in the moment.

- For these times, the Sacred Pause practice can help you to breathe, relax and come back to your centre in only a few moments.

- When you have to make a decision 'on the fly', taking a Sacred Pause first can help you to decide from a place of power and connection with yourself.

A question to think about...

Which Sacred Pause techniques work best for you in which situations?

Final Thoughts

Other Things to Consider

_____

Your energetic diet

Several other factors can affect your energy, which – in turn – will affect your ability to make clear, confident decisions.

In this chapter, we'll look at a few of the most significant elements that make up your 'energetic diet', which includes everything you energetically consume each day. (See the exercise below for specific examples of what goes into your energetic diet.)

If your overall energetic diet supports your energy system and aligns with your truth, you'll be able to connect with and trust your intuition more easily. That trust then helps you to make a decision more quickly and easily.

If your energetic diet disempowers you, however, it will dull your connection with your intuition. You'll find it harder to connect with and trust the messages from your soul. And of course, that will mess with your ability to make good decisions.

Exercise: Rating the quality of your energetic diet

Rate the following aspects of your energetic diet on a scale of 0 to 10, where:

- 0 means you feel awful, disconnected from your truth and full of fear and judgement in this area.
- 10 means this area is in total alignment with your highest good, keeping you fully connected to your intuition and confidently acting on your inspirations.

Physical basics

Examples include food and drink, sleep, fresh air and movement.

Ask yourself:

- Do you mostly eat foods that nourish you or foods that your intuition knows don't support you?
- How much sleep do you get? Is it enough, or do you regularly feel physically tired?
- Do you get out of the house and breathe fresh air (or at least open the windows), or do you only breathe stale or recycled air?
- How often do you move your body? Is movement a joy, or does it feel like a chore?

Give yourself a rating out of 10 for this area.

Emotional health

Examples include connection, friends and family, emotions and feelings.

Ask yourself:

- Are you in relationships with reliable people that you can trust to look out for your highest good, or do you have to 'manage' yourself and the relationship?

- Do you feel a deep sense of connection in your relationships, or are they superficial?

- Is it easy for you to express your emotions, or do you find yourself holding them in?

- Do you trust your feelings, or do you feel safer only using reason and logic to navigate the world?

Give yourself a rating out of 10 for this area.

Information balance

Examples include books, newspapers and magazines, education and learning, TV / movies and social media.

Ask yourself:

- Do the books, newspapers and magazines you read raise your vibration and make you feel hopeful and joyful, or do they leave you feeling hopeless?

- Do you allow yourself to learn new things and follow your curiosity, or do you need a specific reason to learn something new?

- Do the social media pages or channels you follow uplift, inform or inspire you, or do they leave you feeling that you and your life aren't good enough?
- How do you feel after you finish the majority of movies and TV shows you watch?

Give yourself a rating out of 10 for this area.

Spiritual health

Examples include connection to a higher source, sacred ritual, meditation and prayer.

Ask yourself:

- Do you have a deep trust in something bigger than yourself, or do you try to control outcomes and other people?
- Do you perform any sacred rituals to bring you a sense of spiritual connection in your life?
- Do you have a regular meditation practice that clears your mind and helps you to find some inner peace and calm?
- Do you have a prayer practice, or a practice where you connect with or talk to something greater than yourself?

Give yourself a rating out of 10 for this area.

Energetic health

Examples include your SACRED practice, journaling practice, essential oils, herbs, crystals and spending time in nature.

Ask yourself:

- Do you regularly prioritise your energetic health, or is it something you leave for 'when you have enough time' or during emergencies?
- Do you have a journaling practice that helps you to release all that's on your mind?
- Do you work with allies such as essential oils, herbs and crystals to support your energy system?
- Do you make time to be in nature so you can balance your energy and feel grounded?

Give yourself a rating out of 10 for this area.

What changes do you need to make?

Finally, once you've rated yourself in each of these areas, it's time to decide what you want to do with this information. Ask yourself:

- What areas and/or activities prevent you from accessing and trusting your intuition?
- What activities support you in accessing and trusting your intuition?
- What do you need to stop or start doing to help you access and trust your intuition more?
- What do you need to nourish and continue doing to continue accessing and trusting your intuition?

Use the answers to these questions to make changes in your daily life that will support your energetic health and connect you to your intuition.

These will be vital pieces of information to help you to 'ditch your doubt' and make clear, confident decisions that truly benefit you.

If you discover lots of areas that need improvement, just focus on one of them to start with. Trying to address all of them at once is a surefire recipe for more overwhelm. You can always choose a new area once you're comfortable with your changes in the first one.

Or you could choose a new area each week, or even each month.

As I've said a few times in the book now, looking after your energy system is like going to the gym. Yes, working out sporadically is better than not doing it at all... but you'll lose most of the benefits you've gained before your next workout. As a result, you'll constantly be starting again from zero.

If you just make a little more effort a little more frequently, you'll keep building on your previous progress. So, over time, you'll build up your resilience and strength.

And the bonus of these sacred practices is that you can do them from the comfort of your own home – no bulky equipment needed!

If you'd like some more inspiration on how to create a Sacred Pause in your day, come and visit my shop at www. RebeccaAnuwen.com/the-shop. I've created everything in the shop – from meditations to energy clearings, journals, oracle decks and Charm Casting sets – specifically to give you that moment of Sacred Pause.

Conclusion

And that's how you 'ditch the doubt'

Congratulations! You now have all of the tools you need to 'ditch the doubt', create clarity and feel great about your decisions every time.

Any time you have a choice to make, you have access to a whole toolkit of ideas that move you from doubt and confusion into clarity and confidence about your decisions. That means:

- no more worrying about making the wrong decision
- no more doubting yourself or constantly changing your mind
- no more sitting on the fence, wasting your time and energy
- no more feeling paralysed by indecision

Instead, you'll know exactly what you want and what best aligns with you, your goals and your vision for your life. You'll be able to weave your logic and reason in together WITH the intuitive messages you receive when your energy is flowing clearly.

That means you'll get the best of both worlds – and so will your decisions. And more than that, you'll discover a new-found belief in yourself and your ability to confidently see those decisions through.

Additionally, you'll know how to best create space in your life.

You'll have the SACRED practice to use in the morning to start your day fresh, grounded and energetically aligned. That will help you to distinguish all the voices, messages, ideas and energies that are yours from those that aren't... And, as a result, you'll be able to make clear, conscious choices for the day ahead.

You'll also have the GRACE practice to bring closure to your day or week. It will help you to let go of everything you've accumulated that isn't yours. It will also allow you to recognise and reflect on all that you've done (or chosen not to do). That will ensure you can start the next day or week with an energetic reset that leaves you feeling refreshed, calm and clear.

And finally, you'll have the Sacred Pause – a quick, simple, in-the-moment practice that you can use anywhere at any time you need to create space in your life.

You don't have to take this journey alone

As I've mentioned before, these are practices. That means they need practising – and the more you practise them, the more effective they become.

So now is the *perfect* time to choose a practice to start with and actually do it.

You might choose one practice and just focus on that for a few days or weeks. Then, when you feel completely comfortable with it and it's become part of your routine, you can pick the next practice to try.

Or you might want to jump right in with both feet, and add all three practices into your routine.

Regardless, do whatever works for you. Just make sure that you do *something*.

If you can't decide where to start, that's a clear indication that you really DO NEED this book! So, for the first and only time, I'll make that decision for you: I suggest you start with the SACRED practice.

Now that I've chosen for you, I'll hand the baton off to you. As I do, I'll remind you that every decision on how you move forward from here is yours to make. At first, that responsibility may feel a little scary. But I promise, after you're regularly using these practices and you've 'ditched the doubt', that fear will transform into liberation. You'll feel empowered and excited as you suddenly realise that decisions are now your gateway to possibility and potential.

And if you 'fall off the wagon' and wake up one day to discover that you've not done any of the practices for a while, that's okay. Just pick up the book again or head over to www.RebeccaAnuwen.com/DecisionBonuses to be inspired and start over again.

You can also follow me on Instagram on @themodernwitchway, where I share content to remind you how powerful you are and how to keep 'ditching the doubt'.

Or, if you'd like some weekly inspiration, head over to my website www.RebeccaAnuwen.com and sign up for my newsletter. It's full of hints, tips and stories of how to live a more magical, aligned life.

Finally, if you'd like more resources to help you connect with your truth or keep your energy flowing beautifully, or to work with me in a deeper way, visit www.RebeccaAnuwen.com/the-shop.

A few last thoughts...

As you finish this book, I want you to know that it's more than okay for you to prioritise your wants, needs and desires. It's more than okay to take up space in the world with your thoughts, your feelings, your physicality and your decisions.

In fact, it's essential.

It's essential because – remember – you *are* the magic. There's no-one in the world like you and that is your magic.

The world is a little dimmer when you don't give yourself permission to show up fully. It's a little less interesting when you don't allow yourself to make the choices that light you up and express the truth of who you are.

Embrace yourself, embrace life and embrace your decisions with a new-found confidence.

My one hope is that you'll make the huge, life-changing and world-changing decision to show up more fully and be more you!

With love, magic and wishes for clear decisions from now on

Rebecca

Who is The Modern Witch?

Why the Modern Witch Way?

There's no question that the word 'Witch' is emotive.

For many people, it will conjure up the archetypal fairytale image of an evil old woman who causes trouble and uses her magic to harm. For others, a Witch may be a powerful woman who lives on her own terms in harmony with the cycles of life.

Many women who were (and are still) labelled as 'Witches' were those who spoke up and went against expectations and societal norms. They were labelled as 'too much'. And today, there's still a fear of being 'too much' – perhaps because we don't want to fall prey to the historical persecution of Witches in times gone by.

The accusation of being 'too much' is still used to keep us silent – silent about injustices, silent about our own needs and silent in our own choices. Perhaps that's why Witches can also symbolise all that's wild, powerful and unapologetic.

That can scare many people, including other women who want to be all of those things.

It's not about wearing black pointy hats...

The modern-day Witch is less about old stereotypes, and much more about remembering and reclaiming the truth of who you are.

When you reclaim this truth, you get to celebrate your wild edges, not just the socially acceptable 'pretty' parts. You can also reclaim your inner power, so that you can know exactly who you are and stand by what's important to you.

This is a truth where you can be unapologetic in your choices. You can say, "Yes," without explanation and, "No," without apology.

This may mean breaking down old paradigms of belief. It may mean working outside of all that you've been taught about what's right and wrong, good and bad, expected and acceptable.

And yes, it may mean being labelled 'too much'.

But when you honour yourself, your energy and what's important to you, other people's opinions don't stop you from doing what you know you need to. Nor do they stop you from making the decisions that are right for you.

So the modern-day Witch is a woman who's ready to reclaim her power and create change in her world. She's a woman who seeks inner authority, progress, healing and change.

Pleased to meet you – I'm a modern-day Witch

I've chosen to powerfully claim the title 'Witch' when it would've been far easier to choose the more acceptable title of 'Priestess'. I am, after all, a trained Priestess of Cerridwen, which required two years of training in Glastonbury, UK.

But what I found was that the term Priestess feels 'safe'. It certainly isn't threatening in any way, because a Priestess is 'in service' to others and her community.

Witches, on the other hand, are often solitary, and seen as only out for themselves.

It's still not socially acceptable for a woman to prioritise herself and her needs. She still risks being called selfish if she focusses on herself, especially if she says, "No." She's still shunned if she's 'full of herself', and looked at with suspicion if she chooses to walk her own path.

So here I am, Rebecca Anuwen, modern-day Witch, Kinesiologist and Priestess of Cerridwen, reminding you that it's essential for you to also embody YOUR modern-day Witch self. Only then can you 'ditch the doubt' and remind yourself of what's truly important to you. Only then can you break free of the distractions and energy drains of guilt, expectations and judgements.

I'm Rebecca Anuwen, a spell-breaking, story-weaving, wand-wielding, cloak-wearing eternal optimist who laughs at her own jokes and is obsessed with trees.

I love to work with people who are ready to break free of limitations and expectations to express themselves fully and joyously in a way that's meaningful to them.

I believe it's time to break the spell of societal expectations and walk our own paths. It's time to choose where those paths are heading and decide for ourselves what 'Happily Ever After' looks like.

It's good to meet you!

It's good to meet ALL of you, in all of your fullness – in your beautiful, complicated, messy, imperfectly perfect self.

I hope that by now, at the very end of this book, you're more 'full of yourself' than you were at the start. And I hope too that you're ready to fill yourself up even more – to 'ditch the doubt', create clarity and feel good about your decisions every time!

SACRED Practice
Quick Reference Guide

- **STRIP** off all of your jewellery and crystals, so you can feel YOU. Feel how your energy flows naturally, and notice where your 'edges' are.

- **ALIGN** your energy, using simple practices to remove anything that isn't yours or that no longer serves you. Bring yourself back to your centre and connect with your own truth.

- **CONNECT** with your Higher Self, your inner-most knowing, to receive any messages it might have for you (and help you to trust anything you receive).

- **ROOT** into your true essence, so that you're grounded and present.

- **ENCIRCLE** yourself with your energetic shield, supporting your boundaries to keep out whatever isn't yours and protect whatever is.

- **DECIDE** what you want to experience during the coming day / week / month, and then draw that to you with powerful, aligned intentions.

GRACE Practice
Quick Reference Guide

- **GROUND** your energy and become present to bring closure to the energy of the day or week, and get ready to confidently move forward.

- **RECOGNISE** all that you've done, achieved and consciously chosen not to do during the day or week, and savour your accomplishments so you can build on them.

- **APPRECIATE** yourself and take time to really honour who you are and how you've shown up in the world over the past day or week.

- **CALL BACK YOUR ENERGY** from external people, events or situations, so that you can move forward without letting the past influence your thoughts and decisions.

- **EMBODY** your truth, and become so full of your dreams and desires that you leave no room for other people's expectations and judgements.

Printed in Great Britain
by Amazon

59168405R00092